COPYCAT COOKBOOK:

Making at Home Your Favorite Recipes from
the Most Popular Restaurants. A Simple and Accurate Step-By-Step
Guide with Over 100 Tasty Dishes for Your Delicious Meals

Amber Hawkins

TABLE OF CONTENTS

Introduction

Tired of paying for expensive drinks and other food items at Starbucks? Yes, we love them too, but does it not feel like a pain to go to the store. Not to mention all the traffic jams and the crowd at the shop.

In reading this, you will realize that you can cook at home the recipes that you love the most for a fraction of the cost of dining out. You will find step-by-step directions for all those amazing dishes that draw people into restaurants, and you will be sure that the food was cooked under hygienic conditions since you will be making it yourself.

You don't have to be a master chef to prepare these meals. All these recipes use basic ingredients that can be found in any grocery store.

In this cookbook, you can find copycat recipes that look and taste just like those from Starbucks and other restaurants. If you think there is a secret in making these, yes there is, but guess what, we have broken the code. Now, everyone, including you can enjoy these foods and drinks in the comfort of their own home.

Cooking in itself is a form of therapy and you learn an amazing and vital skill set along the way! An exciting journey awaits you in this book! Get ready to learn some tasty, fantastically easy, and fun recipes for all times of the day. And the little cherry on top? We've added in some scrumptious special recipes that will taste just like your favorite restaurant meals!

Get ready to enjoy mouthwatering copycat recipes you are sure to love!

What are Copycat Recipes

Many restaurant recipes aren't special or made with secret ingredients, many of their hottest dishes are classic dishes we already know and love.

Each copycat restaurant recipe needs a couple of tricks up its sleeve. Presentation and selection of the best vegetables for your platter are essential considerations. Of course, most of these tips apply whether you're recreating your favorite restaurant meal or cooking your favorite family recipe. Presentation is of equal importance to taste.

Here are a few tips on how to present your dishes to impress them:

- If served on white plates, the food looks more appetizing.
- Make sure the plate's rim is clean after placing the food on it. Use a new, moist clean cloth always to clean the surface.
- Arrange the food clearly and neatly on the tray.

- Most people never use their finest cutlery. Take out the best possible cutlery for maximum effect.
- Select foods, so you get a variety of colors on the plate.
- A garnish on top of the main meal gives a professional look to the platter. A small portion of basil atop a pasta dish, for example.
- If a sauce is included in your dish, then pour a moderate amount on each plate and add a small jug.

It is essential to buy fresh vegetables, both for appearance and taste. Once you know what to look for, it's easy to choose quality vegetables.

- Select luminous green asparagus with a firm, closed tips. Look for the vibrant green color, covering most spear.
- Search for firm beets with a vibrant deep red color. The root is built to be slender.
- Use broccoli with strong but sturdy stalks. The buds should be closed tightly, and the leaves should be green and crisp.
- Of solid, fresh, and crispy leaves, pick cabbages. Heads should be secure and lightweight.

Getting into the habit of eating at home is a hard thing but learning how to cook your favorite restaurant meals in the comfort of your kitchen can make it a little easier. It's not that hard to learn how to cook secret restaurant meals. People think you need a background in cooking or a degree in culinary arts to be able to cook those secret dishes.

Advantages of Cooking at Home over-eating Outside

What better way to control the consistency of what you and your family shove into your mouth than by preparing your meals? Today, this remains the best reason to learn to cook because you can.

If you cook regularly already at home, you reap plenty of the physical, mental, and social benefits of eating nutritious food from scratch. You may often want to check some of the health benefits of home cooking if you eat out all the time.

Saving money is one of the advantages of home cooking

During your work lunchtime, your paycheck will be drained by fast food or diner. You will get 10 dollars or more from a quick lunch at the restaurant. When you eat out five days a week, 20 days a month, a large amount of food that will destroy your health will disappear. Although an occasional dinner or pizza delivery is not so much a cash drain for most people, eating out once or twice a day is a burden on finances. Cooking at home gives you plenty of tasty leftovers for lunch tomorrow. According to this Time magazine report, brown-bagging your lunch can save you $2,500 per year.

SAVING TIME IS A HUGE BENEFIT OF HOME COOKING.

The food routine is like this – driving to the restaurant, waiting for the order, waiting for the food, dining, waiting to pay, and driving home. The time taken to prepare, serve, and consume a home-cooked meal may be up to two hours.

TOGETHER WITH THE FAMILY

In the rapid digital age of this day, families eat either on the go or while watching the television or the phone. Not exactly the easiest way to communicate with relatives. Take a sense of camaraderie and prepare and eat meals together.

HOMEMADE FOODS HELP YOU TO EAT FOR LONGER

Research has shown that people are more likely to live longer cooking at home five days a week, according to the elderly Taiwanese people. Frequent cooking helps women more than men, and longevity has been attributed to other factors such as eating less and exercising at least twice a week. In your golden years, the benefits of home cooking will keep you safe and energetic.

GOOD MEALS IN THE DIET

The benefits of home cooking include consuming more nutritious foods. You can increase the vitamin and mineral content of meals with fresh seafood, poultry, and butcher cuts from a supermarket and fruits and vegetables from a farmer's market. Home cooking increases the amounts of vitamins B6, B6, A, B12, and E, which you consume, and also reduces the saturated fat content of foods.

HOMEMADE FOODS LOWER CALORIE, FAT, AND SODIUM

If you want to sustain or even lose your current weight, home cooking allows you to reduce food intake by at least 140 calories a day. Also, if you prepare the meal, you usually use less sugar, salt, butter, and oil than a skilled chef at a restaurant.

FOOD SATISFACTION – MEALS ARE MORE ENJOYABLE WHEN COOKING AT HOME

The purchase of food, food planning, and cooking (with or without your family's or significant others' assistance) reinforces the value of certain foods. It encourages you to think more about portions and calories. This will reduce food consumption and encourage you to choose foods based on taste and economy rather than order anything quick from a limited menu.

IMPROVED FOOD HEALTH

E. coli, listeria, salmonella, and other eating-borne illnesses found in restaurant foods and prepackaged meals impact millions of Americans each year. You won't know how the ingredients have been processed, prepared, and treated while cooking or dining in a restaurant. If you are dining at a restaurant, you won't know if they hold the level of cleanliness between the inspections. You monitor your food, cooking times, and temperatures at home to relax and make sure you eat properly.

Zero Additives

When you dine at restaurants or eat processed foods, you can never be sure of all the ingredients that have been used in the food. The majority of the time, the food items tend to contain a significant percentage of chemical additives, added sugar, excessive calories, and unhealthy fat that can hamper your health.

Controlling the Ingredients To Be Used

The moment you decide on cooking your food at home, you can exercise full control over the ingredients in the food. So, when you think that a particular ingredient is not good or healthy, you can easily omit it. However, when you opt for dining at restaurants, nothing can be done to eliminate the calorific or unhealthy ingredients added to the food. Cooking the same dishes at home will help you maintain a healthy diet. You will be able to meet all your goals of losing weight while enjoying all your favorite cuisines. It will help in boosting your level of energy. You will be feeling a lot healthier besides looking fit.

Controlling Portions

When you go to a restaurant, you will not be able to control the food portions you want to consume. The reason behind this is that the restaurant will be serving you a fixed portion of food, and that is usually more than what the human body needs. Moreover, most famous and well-known restaurants will be serving you food that is twice or even thrice the recommended guidelines of any diet.

Consumes Less Time

If you have the notion that cooking food at home will take up a lot of time that you cannot afford, you need to think again. It will not be taking up much time as you think if you can plan everything accordingly. You will be finding various easy, tasty, and healthy recipes from all over the world in this book that you can cook even during the weekdays. On the other hand, when you think of eating outside, you will need to wait to get your reservation, order the desired food, and wait for the preparation, and then, after a long time, your meal will be served to you. So, as you can see, it is a long process.

Great Family Time

There is no need to be an accomplished chef for cooking tasty meals. No one is born with any skill. Everyone learns it along the way. All you need is some practice, along with the desire to cook some great meals that will make the whole process a lot easier.

When you cook meals at home, you can turn it into a family-based activity for spending more quality time with the members of your family. It will help in replenishing your mental health as well. For those parents who stay out for work on most days, you can bake desserts, snacks, and cookies with your kids to spend some great time with them.

CHAPTER 1:

Famous Breakfast Recipes

California A.M. Crunch Wrap

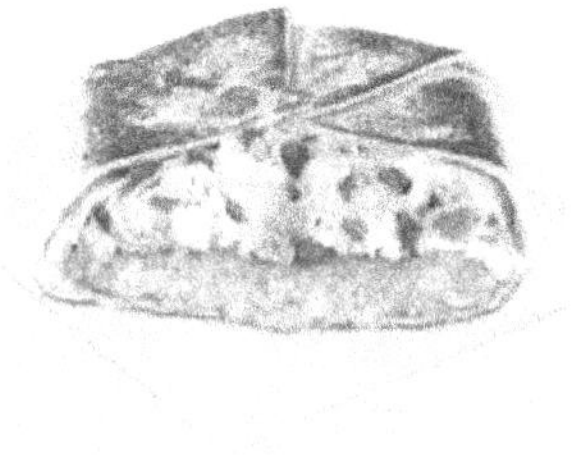

Preparation Time: 10 minutes

Cooking Time: 20 minutes

Servings: 4

Ingredients:

4 frozen hash brown patties

5 large eggs - 1 tablespoon milk

Salt and pepper, to taste - 4 large tortillas

1 cup cheddar cheese, shredded

4 strips of thick-cut bacon, cooked and crumbled

2 ripe California avocados, peeled and pitted

4 tablespoons Pico de Gallo

Directions:

Cook hash brown patties until crisp, based on package directions. Add eggs, milk, salt, and pepper in a bowl. Mix well until combined. Then, pour onto a skillet and cook until scrambled. Set aside.

Heat two different-sized (one smaller than the other) heavy-bottomed pans over medium heat. Once heated, place tortillas into the bigger pan and, in even amounts, add cheese, a hash brown patty, eggs, bacon, avocado, and Pico de Gallo in the center of the tortilla in that order. Using a wheel pattern, fold the tortilla around the filling with the edge facing up. Place heated smaller pan (such as a cast-iron skillet) on top for about 20 seconds or until browned. Serve immediately.

Olive Garden Eggs Benedict with Hollandaise Sauce

Preparation Time: 10 minutes

Cooking Time: 20 minutes

Servings: 4

Ingredients: 8 rashes of bacon

4 eggs

2 tsp of white vinegar

2 English muffins (you can substitute this for other carbs, like rye bread, scones, bagels, etc.)

1 ½ tsp of butter Hollandaise Sauce:

5 tbsp unsalted butter (if you have salted butter, omit the salt from this recipe)

3 egg yolks

1 tbsp of lemon juice

½ tsp salt

dash of cayenne pepper or tabasco

Directions:

Preheat a frying pan on medium heat for your bacon and add a drizzle of oil. Preheat another medium saucepan filled 2/3 up with water to a boil, for your eggs. Once the water is boiling, add in your vinegar and then lower the heat so it begins to simmer.

Place your bacon strips in the frying pan and allow them to fry for about 10 minutes (until crispy brown). While your bacon is frying, crack one egg into the saucepan with water and wait for it to solidify a little. Once you can see the egg starting to gain a nice white circular form, you can add another. Repeat the process until all your eggs are in the pot, then lower the heat and cover the pot with a lid and let it cook for about 4 minutes.

Prep your English muffins – you can either toast them or butter them up. If you prefer a nice greasy breakfast – you can use the same pan that you fried your bacon in, to toast your muffins/bread. It brings a lovely flavor to the muffins, and you save on oil.

Check on your bacon to see if it's crisp – once it is, remove it with a fork and place it on a paper towel (this drains out the excess fat) with a plate under it.

Once your eggs have been cooking for about 4 minutes, gently scoop them out with a sieve or a slotted spoon, so that you drain out excess water and place them over the English muffins.

Now for the Hollandaise sauce: melt your 5 tbsp of butter. In a blender (if you don't have a blender, you can whisk these ingredients together), combine the 3 egg yolks, lemon juice, cayenne, and salt and blend for 20 seconds until the mixture looks a light pale yellow. Then lower your mixing speed, and drizzle in your butter.

Once mixed, dollop the Hollandaise sauce over your eggs and serve with bacon.

FETA FRITTATA

Preparation Time: 5 minutes

Cooking Time: 15 minutes

Servings: 6

Ingredients: 6 eggs

¼ cup of milk

2 garlic cloves/1 tsp garlic paste

¼ tsp salt & ¼ tsp pepper

½ tsp chili flakes - ¼ onion, chopped

2 scallions, diced - 2 cups of broccoli

¼ cup of Feta cheese

a handful of seeds (optional)

1 tbsp oil

Directions:

Drizzle the oil into a small pan over medium heat. Toss in your onions, scallions, chili flakes, and salt and pepper, and fry them.

In a separate bowl, combine your eggs, milk, garlic, and a pinch of salt and pepper, and whisk well. Preheat your oven to 400°F and lightly grease a baking dish (8x8 dish is best suited). Once the onions in the pan begin to brown a little, add in your broccoli and cook for about 5 minutes – then slowly pour the egg mixture into the pan, add in some seeds and lightly stir, just to even out the contents.

Next, pour the contents from the pan into the baking dish and crumble Feta cheese over the top. Pop the dish in the oven and bake for 20 minutes.

Cracker Barrel Savory Muffins

Preparation Time: 10 minutes

Cooking Time: 15 minutes

Servings: 6

Ingredients:

4 eggs

200g spinach

¼ tomato

½ cup of mixed veg stir fry or):

cup of corn

¼ cup of peas

100g green beans

¼ red onion

200g cheddar cheese

1 tsp salt

1 tsp cayenne pepper

½ tsp chili flakes

1 tsp garlic & herb paste

1 tbsp olive oil

1 tbsp butter

Directions:

Drizzle olive oil into a skillet/pan over medium heat.

Dice the tomato, cheese, and onion and finely chop the spinach and green beans.

Use the butter to grease a muffin tray and preheat your oven to 400° F.

Crack the eggs into the pan, add your salt, pepper, chili flakes, and garlic & herb paste and carefully whisk the mixture together until light and fluffy.

Add in all the vegetables and cheese and give the mixture one last stir, before evenly pouring the mixture into 6 of the cups in the muffin tray – each cup should be about ¾ filled with the mixture.

Pop the tray in the oven and bake for 15

20 minutes.

HAM & CHEESE OMELET: DENNY'S COPYCAT

Preparation time: 5 minutes

Cooking time: 15 minutes

Serving: 1

Ingredients:

1 tbsp. Butter

3 Eggs

3 tbsp. Water (

a pinch of each Salt and black pepper

.5 cup Shredded Swiss cheese

.5 cup Fully cooked cubed ham

Directions:

Warm a skillet using the med-high temperature setting.

Whisk the eggs, salt, pepper, and water, and pour into the skillet to scramble.

When the eggs are set, add the ham with a sprinkle of cheese.

APPLEBEE WHOLE WHEAT PANCAKES

Preparation Time: 15 minutes

Cooking Time: 20 minutes

Serving: 6

Ingredients:

1 ½ cups of milk (alternatively you can use oat/soy milk)

¼ cup of white vinegar

2 large free-range eggs

¼ cup of oil

¼ cup of honey (golden/maple syrup is also a good substitute)

2 ½ cups of whole wheat flour

1 tsp baking soda

1 tsp baking powder

1 tsp cinnamon

¼ salt

oil (or butter) to lightly grease your pan

Directions:

Pour the vinegar and milk into a bowl and gently stir the mixture. Leave the mixture to stand for about 10 minutes – it should start to curdle and become "buttermilk".

While you allow the mixture to stand, you can preheat your pan to medium-high heat.

Whisk the eggs, oil, honey, baking soda, baking powder, cinnamon, and salt into your buttermilk mixture, making sure it is well combined.

Gently sift the flour into the mixture and stir well with a spatula/wooden spoon, breaking down all the lumps.

Once your pan is hot enough, lightly drizzle some oil/butter to evenly coat the surface of the pan (make sure the oil sizzles, so your pancakes can fry nicely).

Using a spoon/cup, pour your mixture into the pan, creating circular shapes – you can decide how big/small you'd like your pancakes to be.

Allow the mixture to fry for 3-4 minutes (you should start seeing bubbles appear in the mixture or browning around the circumference). Flip the pancakes and cook for another minute.

Repeat the process until your batter is done – remember to adjust the heat of your pan accordingly:

Since the oil is now hot, it may burn your pancakes if you leave the heat on too high.

Voila!

You've made perfect, fluffy, and healthy pancakes that will keep you feeling full!

You can add your touches of green yogurt, honey, berries – whatever you fancy for that day!

If you have any leftovers, you can always pop them in the freezer and reheat them out throughout the week!

Red Lobster Dark Chocolate & Cinnamon Quinoa Bowl

Preparation Time: 5 minutes

Cooking Time: 25 minutes

Serving: 6

Ingredients:

1 cup of uncooked quinoa

1 cup of almond milk (alternatively you can use soy/oat/rice milk)

1 cup of coconut milk

a pinch of salt

a pinch of cinnamon

2 tbsp of cocoa powder

2-3 tbsp of honey

3-4 squares of dark chocolate

1 banana

a handful of raisins/berries (optional)

Directions:

Place a pan on medium heat.

While the pan heats up, rinse your quinoa for about 2 minutes and then strain it out.

Pour the washed quinoa into the pan and allow it to slightly toast.

Add your almond milk, coconut milk, and salt into the pot and slowly mix the ingredients. Raise the heat and bring to boil, then lower the heat, allowing the pot to simmer for about 20-25 minutes, stirring frequently. Once the quinoa has absorbed the liquid, remove the pot from the hot plate and mix in your cocoa powder, honey, and cinnamon. You can add in more almond milk if you'd fancy a more milky texture.

Chop up your banana and chocolate squares and mix them into your bowl. Add raisins/berries if you have any. You can refrigerate the quinoa for up to 2-3 days if you have any leftovers, and add in more almond milk when reheating it, to bring back the moistness.

Scram Slam: Denny's Copycat

Preparation time: 10 minutes

Cooking time: 15 minutes

Serving: 2

Ingredients:

1 slice white onion

¼ of 1 Green bell pepper

4 Mushrooms

1.5 tbsp. Butter

6Eggs

as desired Salt

On the Side:

Hash browns

Sausage

Bacon

Directions:

Dice the pepper and onion. Slice the mushrooms. Toss the prepared veggies with one tablespoon of butter into a skillet using the medium heat setting until they're tender (5 min.), Prepare another skillet with the rest of the butter (medium temp). Whisk and scramble the eggs (5-7 min.). Add the cheese and stir in the peppers, mushrooms, and onions with a dash of salt. Serve the eggs with chopped tomatoes and your chosen sides.

McDonald's' Fruit and Yogurt Parfait

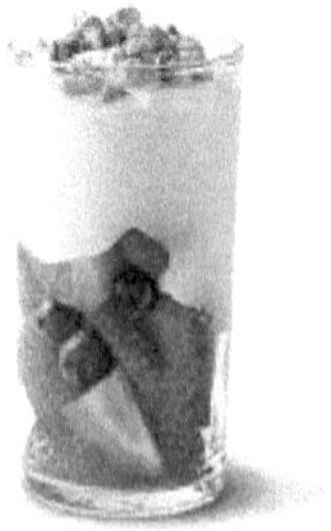

Preparation time: 5 minutes

Cooking time: 20 minutes

Serving: 10

Ingredients:

6 ounces vanilla yogurt, divided into 3

4–6 strawberries, sliced

¼ cup blueberries, fresh or frozen; divided into 2

¼ cup pecans, chopped; divided into 2

Directions:

Place 2 ounces of vanilla yogurt at the bottom of a cup, followed by 2–3 strawberries and ⅛ cup of blueberries and pecans.

Place another layer of yogurt, strawberries, blueberries, and pecans on top of the first layer.

Finish off the parfait with the remaining yogurt—you can garnish it with more fruits if you like.

CHAPTER 2:

Appetizers and Snacks Recipes

PEI WEI SWEET RESTAURANT SLAW

Preparation time: 5 minutes

Cooking time: 20 minutes

Serving: 10

Ingredients

2 **tbsps.** diced onion

3 **tbsps.** vegetable oil

1/2 cup white sugar

1 **tbsp.** white vinegar

1/4 **tsp.** salt

1/2 **tsp.** poppy seeds

Direction

In a big bowl, stir the onion and coleslaw mix together.

Beat poppy seeds, salt, vinegar, sugar, vegetable oil, and salad dressing together in a mid-sized bowl until entirely combined. Empty this into the big bowl. Coat everything by tossing. Before serving, leave it chilling for a minimum of 2 hours first.

AMY'S LETTUCE WRAPS

Preparation time: 5 minutes

Cooking time: 30 minutes

Serving: 10

Ingredients

Dipping Sauce:

1/2 cup water

1/4 cup white sugar

2 **tbsps.** soy sauce

2 **tbsps.** rice vinegar

2 **tbsps.** ketchup

1 **tbsp.** lemon juice

1/8 **tsp.** sesame oil

Hot Mustard:

1 **tbsp.** dry mustard

2 **tsps.** water, divided

Stir-Fry Sauce:

2 **tbsps.** soy sauce

2 **tbsps.** brown sugar

1/2 **tsp.** rice vinegar

Filling:

3 **tbsps.** peanut oil, divided

1 **lb.** ground pork

1 cup minced water chestnuts

8 **oz.** chopped fresh mushrooms

3 **tbsps.** chopped green onion

1 **tsp.** minced garlic

To Serve:

1 head iceberg lettuce

1 **tsp.** red chile paste, or more to taste

Direction

In a small microwavable bowl, mix white sugar and 1/2 cup water. Warm in microwave for 30 seconds to dissolve the sugar. Put sesame oil, lemon juice, ketchup, 2 **tbsps.** rice vinegar and 2 **tbsps.** soy sauce; combine till dipping sauce is blended thoroughly. Cover using plastic wrap and refrigerate for 30 minutes.

Mix several drops of water and dry mustard. Add in the rest of the water till the mixture resembles the consistency of hot mustard.

In a small bowl, mix 1/2 **tsp.** rice vinegar, brown sugar, and 2 **tbsps.** soy sauce to create stir-fry sauce.

In a big skillet or wok, heat 2 **tbsps.** of peanut oil over high heat. Put the pork; cook and mix for 5 minutes till browned. Put the garlic, green onions, mushrooms, water chestnuts, and rest of the 1 **tbsp.** oil; sauté for 2 minutes till flavors incorporate. Add in stir-fry sauce; mix for 3 to 4 minutes to cover the pork mixture equally.

Cut out the stem of lettuce and rinse well. Get rid of the outer leaf. Cautiously remove whole leaves and halve lengthwise. Set on a paper-towels-lined-plate.

Into ramekins or small bowls, spoon dipping sauce. Add in red chili paste and hot mustard to preferred level of spiciness. Into the lettuce halves, scoop the pork filling and roll it up; put dipping sauce on top or dip wraps.

McDonald Taco Bell Seasoning Copycat

Preparation time: 5 minutes

Cooking time: 40 minutes

Serving: 10

Ingredients

1 **tbsp.** dried onion flakes

1 **tsp.** all-purpose flour

1 **tsp.** beef bouillon granules

1 **tsp.** garlic salt

1 **tsp.** ground cumin

1/4 **tsp.** cayenne pepper

1/4 **tsp.** white sugar

Direction

In a bowl, mix sugar, cayenne pepper, chili powder, paprika, cumin, garlic salt, beef bouillon, flour, and onion flakes.

Panera Take-out Fake-out Pollo Con Crema

Preparation time: 5 minutes

Cooking time: 40 minutes

Serving: 10

Ingredients

4 large skinless, boneless chicken breast halves

cubed

salt and pepper to taste

2 **tbsps.** extra virgin olive oil, divided

1 (8 **oz.**) package sliced fresh mushrooms

2 large red bell peppers, cut into chunks

1 large yellow onion, sliced

2 cloves garlic, minced

1/4 cup butter

1/4 cup all-purpose flour

1 1/2 cups low-sodium chicken broth

1 1/2 cups heavy cream

1/4 cup sour cream

3 **tbsps.** ketchup, or to taste

2 dashes hot pepper sauce

(such as Frank's RedHot®), or to taste

1 **tsp.** ground cumin

1/2 **tsp.** ground dried Anaheim or California chiles (optional)

12 (6 inch) flour tortillas

Direction

Sprinkle pepper and salt on chicken cubes. Heat 1 tbsp. olive oil in a big skillet on medium heat; mix and cook for 5-10 minutes till chicken juices run clear.

Put the chicken in the bowl.

Heat 1 tbsp. olive oil in a skillet on medium heat; mix and cook garlic, onions, bell peppers, and mushrooms for 10 minutes till veggies start to brown.

Put veggies in a bowl with chicken.

Melt butter on medium-high heat in the same skillet; whisk the flour in. Cook mixture for 2 minutes till roux gives off toasted fragrant and lightly browned; whisk broth in. Simmer; whisk till thick.

Lower heat to low; whisk ground dried chiles, cumin, hot sauce, ketchup, sour cream, and cream in.

Cover; simmer for 15 minutes till flavors blend and thick, occasionally mixing.

Mix veggies and chicken in gently; serve rolled in the flour tortillas.

TEXAS ROADHOUSE HOT WIENER SAUCE

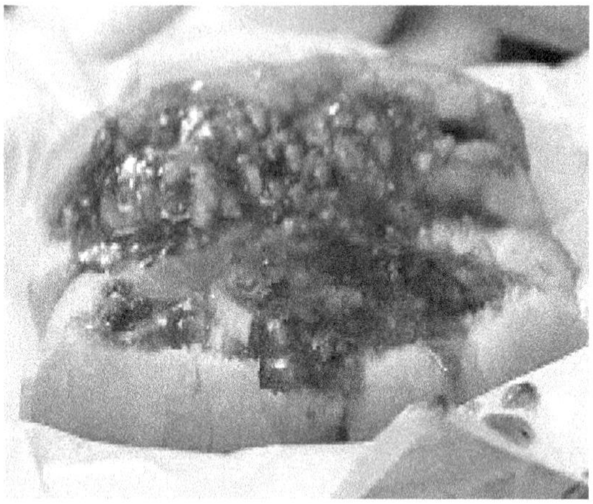

Preparation time: 5 minutes

Cooking time: 20 minutes

Serving: 10

Ingredients

6 cups water

1/2 **lb.** all-beef hot dogs, ground

1/4 cup white vinegar

1 **tsp.** sea salt, or more to taste

1 **tsp.** red pepper flakes

1/2 **tsp.** onion powder

1/2 **tsp.** dried oregano

1/2 **tsp.** ground cinnamon

1/4 **tsp.** ground white pepper

1/4 **tsp.** dried thyme leaves

2 grinds freshly ground black pepper or more to taste

1/2 cup cornstarch

1/4 cup cold water, or as needed

Direction

Mix a big stockpot with water, vinegar, sea salt, ground hot dogs, paprika, onion powder, chili powder, black pepper, red pepper flakes, cinnamon, oregano, thyme, and white pepper. Boil then bring the heat down to a medium-low then let it simmer for 45 minutes.

Dissolve cornstarch completely in cold water then stir in the hot dog mixture. Let it cook for 15 minutes longer until the sauce has slightly thickened with frequent stirring. Taste mixture and add salt and pepper if needed then serve.

Panera Fried Mac and Cheese Balls

Preparation time:15 minutes

Cooking time 15 minutes

Servings: 6

Ingredients:

Sauce:

1 ¾ cups marinara sauce

1 ¾ cups alfredo sauce

¼ cup heavy whipping cream

1 teaspoon garlic powder

½ cup ricotta cheese

1 cup Italian blend shredded cheese

¼ cup red wine

Balls:

16 ounces grated white sharp cheddar, grated

16 ounces smoked gouda cheese, grated

3 tablespoons butter

2 tablespoons flour

2 cups whole milk, warmed

1-pound large elbow macaroni, cooked

Salt and pepper, to taste

3 eggs

3 tablespoons milk

3 cups panko bread crumbs

Fresh Parmesan cheese for garnish only

vegetable oil for frying

Directions:

Make the balls. In a mixing bowl, combine the shredded cheddar and shredded gouda.

In a large saucepan, melt the butter. Add the flour slowly, whisking until there are no lumps. Gradually add the 2 cups of warm milk.

Whisk until smooth, and continue cooking until the sauce begins to thicken.

When the sauce is thickened, remove it from the heat and gradually mix in the cheddar and gouda cheeses.

Stir until the cheese is melted and incorporated thoroughly.

Add the cooked macaroni and salt and pepper into the cheese sauce and stir well.

Butter a large cake pan and spread the mac and cheese mixture evenly into the pan, then place it in the refrigerator for at least two hours. You want the mixture to set and make it easier to form into balls.

After two hours, remove the tray from the refrigerator and form the mac and cheese into evenly sized balls about 2 inches in diameter.

Cover, and put them in the freezer for at least an hour.

In a small bowl, beat your eggs and 3 tablespoons of milk together.

Place the bread crumbs in a shallow dish.

In a deep skillet or large saucepan, heat enough vegetable oil so that the balls will be covered when you fry them.

When the oil is heated to 350°F, dip each ball in the egg mixture, then the panko crumbs, and drop them into the oil.

Work in batches, and cook until the balls are a nice golden-brown color, about 3–4 minutes. Transfer to the paper towel as they finish cooking to drain.

Make your cheese sauce by combining the marinara and alfredo sauce in a small saucepan.

Heat over medium and when warm, add the ricotta, Italian cheese blend, and wine. Stir to combine.

When the cheeses have melted, remove the pot from the heat and add the garlic powder and heavy cream.

Stir well.

Serve the macaroni balls with the cheese sauce and a sprinkle of Parmesan.

IHOP Cracker Barrel's Biscuits

Preparation Time: 15 minutes

Cooking Time: 8 minutes

Servings: 8

Ingredients:

2 cups self-rising flour

⅓ cup shortening

⅔ cup buttermilk Melted butter, to brush

Directions:

Preheat oven to 450 °F.

In a bowl, mix flour and shortening until the mixture is loose and crumbly. Pour in buttermilk. Mix well.

Sprinkle flour onto a smooth surface and flatten dough on top. Cut dough

into desired shapes using biscuit cutters.

Arrange onto a baking sheet. Place in oven and cook for 8 minutes. Apply melted butter on top using a brush.

Serve.

TGI FRIDAY HEALTHY CRAB & PITA SHELLS

Preparation Time: 5 minutes

Cooking Time: 0 minutes

Servings: 6

Ingredients:

227g imitation crab meat

4 tbsp. cream cheese

3 tbsp. seafood cocktail sauce

½ tsp salt

½ tsp pepper

6 mini pita pockets

2 green onions

Tabasco sauce (for drizzling)

Directions:

Dice the crab meat and mix into a bowl with cream cheese, cocktail sauce, salt, and pepper.

Pour the mixture into the pita pockets.

Chop up green onion and garnish the pockets. Drizzle with tabasco sauce and serve.

PANDA EXPRESS SHRIMP COCKTAIL

Preparation Time: 10 minutes

Cooking Time: 5 minutes

Servings: 1

Ingredients:

4 green onions, chopped

1 lb. cleaned shrimp

½ cup Miracle Whip Dressing (alternatively you can mix Mayonnaise and Paprika).

1 dash of Sriracha/hot sauce

20 endive leaves (you can use lettuce/ any sturdy leaf alternative)

1 tbsp. butter

½ tbsp. garlic paste

½ tsp lemon juice

Directions:

Heat a pan with the butter in it, on medium heat. Once the butter has melted and sizzling, add in your shrimp and garlic paste. Cook for about 5 minutes until the shrimp flesh turns pink.

In a separate bowl mix your dressing and lemon juice, and combine the shrimp once cooked and cooled down to room temperature.

Wash and separate the endive leaves and plate the leaves facing up

so that they create little bowl-like shapes.

Spoon out the shrimp cocktail into the leaves and add a dash of sriracha sauce to each leaf bowl.

TACO BELL CAPRESE CIABATTA

Preparation Time: 5 minutes

Cooking Time: 10 minutes

Servings: 6

Ingredients:

1 loaf of ciabatta bread, halved lengthwise

4 tbsps. of butter

2 tbsp. garlic paste

12 oz. of sliced mozzarella cheese

½ cup of balsamic vinegar

2 sliced tomatoes

salt and pepper to taste

⅓ cup chopped basil

rosemary, to taste

Directions:

Preheat the oven to 400°F.

Layer both halves of the loaf in the oven, with the crust on the bottom, on a baking tray.

Mix in your butter, garlic, salt, and rosemary in a bowl and evenly spread it over the loaf.

Layer the mozzarella slices on the bread

evenly covering the loaf.

Pop the loaf in the oven and bake for 15 minutes (until cheese is melted).

While the bread is toasting, Pour the balsamic vinegar into a small pan and bring to a boil on the stove. Then lower the heat and let it simmer for about 3 minutes (or until the mixture is halved), then remove from heat and set aside.

Once the loaves are done toasting, remove them from the oven and layer some tomato slices on top of the loaves. Drizzle over the balsamic reduction and garnish with rosemary and basil.

Slice the loaves and serve warm.

CHAPTER 3:

Pasta Recipes

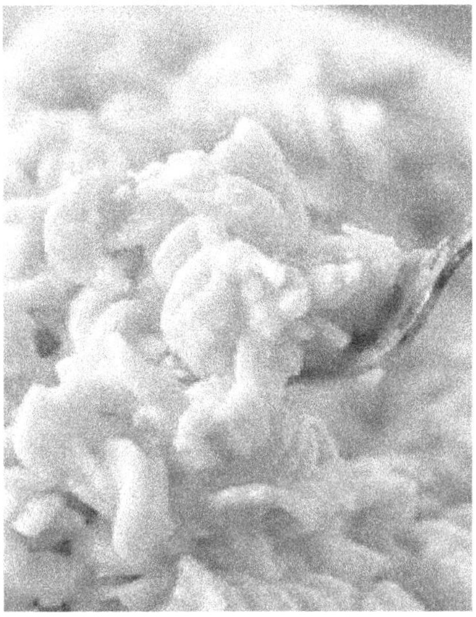

BOSTON MARKET MAC N' CHEESE

Preparation time: 10 minutes

Cooking time: 20minutes

Serving: 6

Ingredients:

1 8-ounce package spiral pasta

2 tablespoons butter

2 tablespoons all-purpose flour

1 ¾ cups whole milk

1 ¼ cups diced processed cheese like Velveeta™

¼ teaspoon dry mustard

½ teaspoon onion powder

1 teaspoon salt

Pepper, to taste

Directions:

Cook pasta according to package directions. Drain then set aside.

To prepare sauce, make the roux with four and butter over medium-low heat in a large deep skillet. Add milk and whisk until well blended. Add cheese, mustard, salt, and pepper. Keep stirring until smooth.

Once pasta is cooked, transfer to a serving bowl. Pour cheese mixture on top. Toss to combine.

Serve warm.

CHILI SPAGHETTI NAPOLITANA

Preparation Time: 5 minutes

Cooking Time: 15 minutes

Serving: 10

Ingredients:

500g dried spaghetti

¼ cup of olive oil

1 tbsp of crushed garlic onion

a pinch of salt and pepper

½ tsp chili powder (optional)

2 curry leaves (optional)

800g of chopped tomato

¼ cup of basil

200g Parmesan cheese (shredded)

Directions:

Bring a large pot filled halfway with water and a pinch of salt, to boil. Add in your spaghetti and leave to cook for about 8-10 minutes.

While the pasta cooks, prepare your Napolitana sauce – heat a pan with a drizzle of oil in it, over medium heat. Add your garlic, onions, salt, pepper, chili powder, and curry leaves into the pan and cook until the onions have browned. Then pour in your tomatoes and ½ a cup of water and leave to simmer for 5 minutes.

Once your spaghetti is cooked, use a colander to drain your pasta and plate it. Pour in your Napolitana sauce, and sprinkle the basil and Parmesan on top.

P.F. CHANG EGGPLANT & OLIVE PASTA SALAD

Preparation Time: 10 minutes

Cooking Time: 20 minutes

Serving: 10

Ingredients:

6 oz of short pasta (such as fusilli/farfalle)

1 eggplant (chopped into ¾ inch squares)

divided tbsp of olive oil

2 tbsp red wine vinegar

1 tsp salt

¼ tsp black pepper

1 tbsp chopped oregano

2 oz of crumbled feta cheese

1 ½ cups of cherry tomatoes, halved

1 cup of pitted olives

Directions:

Set your oven to preheat at 475°F. On a baking tray, lay out the chopped eggplant and olives, and drizzle with 3 tbsp of olive oil. Pop it in the oven and roast for 20 minutes until the eggplant has softened. While the eggplant and olives are roasting, fill a pot halfway with water and a pinch of salt and set the heat to a medium – bringing the water to a boil. Then toss in your pasta and lower the heat to medium-low. Let the pasta simmer for about 10 minutes. In a separate bowl, whisk the vinegar, salt, pepper, oregano, and 3 tbsp of oil together.

Once the pasta has softened, drain it through a colander. Remove the roast vegetables from the oven, once cooked. Mix the pasta, vegetables, crumbled feta, and vinegar mixture in a bowl and garnish with oregano.

Texas Roadhouse Mushroom & Spinach Shells

Preparation Time: 25 minutes

Cooking Time: 40 minutes

Serving: 10

Ingredients:

6 oz of jumbo pasta shells (20 shells)

3 tsp of salt, divided

¾ tsp black pepper

chopped yellow onion

3 tbsp of garlic paste

1 28-oz can of crushed tomatoes

8 oz of mixed sliced wild mushrooms

5 cups of chopped baby spinach

1 16-oz container of whole-milk ricotta cheese

1 cup of grated Parmesan cheese

Directions:

Preheat the oven to 400°F.

Fill a medium pot halfway with water and add a pinch of salt. Place over medium-high heat and bring to a boil. Pour in your pasta shells and lower heat to medium-low. Cook until al-dente – about 7-10 minutes (the pasta shells shouldn't be too soft as they need to also cook in the oven).

While the pasta boils, place 1 tbsp of oil in a separate skillet over medium heat. Add in your onion and garlic and fry until the onions have browned. Add the tomatoes, 1 ½ tsp of salt, and ½ tsp of pepper into the skillet and slowly stir for about 5 minutes until the sauce starts to thicken.

Check on your pasta and drain the shells, using a colander. Set the shells aside to cool down. In another skillet, pour 1 tbsp of oil and bring it to medium heat. Add in the mushrooms, ¼ tsp salt, ½ tsp pepper, and cook for about 5 minutes until the mushrooms have browned. Then add in your spinach and cook for another minute until the spinach is slightly wilted.

In a baking tray, lightly layer the tray with a drizzle of oil and pour the tomato sauce in –

reserve ½ a cup of the sauce for later. Fill the pasta shells with ricotta, mushrooms, and spinach and layer the shells over the tomato sauce, in the baking tray. Pour the remainder ½ cup of tomato over the shells and sprinkle Parmesan cheese over.

Bake for 15 minutes.

Chipotle Macaroni Grill's Pasta Milano

Preparation Time: 5 minutes

Cooking Time: 20 minutes

Servings: 6

Ingredients:

1 pound bowtie pasta

2 teaspoons olive oil

1 pound chicken, chopped into small pieces

1 12-ounce package mushrooms, chopped

1 cup onion, minced

2 garlic cloves, finely minced

½ cup sun-dried tomatoes, diced

1½ cups half and half

1 tablespoon butter, softened

½ cup Parmesan cheese, shredded, plus some more for serving

1 teaspoon black pepper, ground

1 tablespoon fresh basil, minced

Directions:

Follow directions on the package to cook bowtie pasta. Drain then set aside. Add oil to a pan over medium-high heat. Once hot, add chicken and stir-fry for about 5 to 6 minutes until cooked through. Set chicken aside onto a plate. In the same pan, toss in mushrooms, onions, garlic, and sundried tomatoes. Sauté until onions turn soft and mushrooms become a light brown, then sprinkle salt and pepper to season. Return chicken to pan and mix. Mix half and half, butter, Parmesan, pepper, and basil in a small bowl. Add half and half mixture to pan. Stir, and let simmer for about 3 to 4 minutes or until pan ingredients are thoroughly heated. Mix in pasta until coated well.

Serve.

Olive Garden's Fettuccine Alfredo

Preparation Time: 5 minutes

Cooking Time: 25 minutes

Servings: 6

Ingredients:

½ cup butter, melted

2 tablespoons cream cheese

1 pint heavy cream 1 teaspoon garlic powder

Some salt

Some black pepper

⅔ cup parmesan cheese, grated

1 pound fettuccine, cooked

Directions:

Melt the cream cheese in the melted butter over medium heat until soft.

Add the heavy cream and season the mixture with garlic powder, salt, and pepper.

Reduce the heat to low and allow the mixture to simmer for another 15 to 20 minutes. Remove the mixture from heat and add in the parmesan. Stir everything to melt the cheese. Pour the sauce over the pasta and serve.

Cracker Barrel Eggplant & Olive Pasta Salad

Preparation time: 10 minutes

Cooking time: 20 minutes

Serving: 4

Ingredients:

6 oz of short pasta (such as fusilli/farfalle)

1 eggplant (chopped into ¾ inch squares)

6 divided tbsp of olive oil

2 tbsp red wine vinegar

1 tsp salt

¼ tsp black pepper

1 tbsp chopped oregano

2 oz of crumbled feta cheese

1 ½ cups of cherry tomatoes, halved

1 cup of pitted olives

Directions:

Set your oven to temperature at 475°F.

On a baking tray, lay out the chopped eggplant and olives and drizzle with 3 tbsp of olive oil.

Pop it in the oven and roast for 20 minutes until the eggplant has softened.

While the eggplant and olives are roasting, fill a pot halfway with water and a pinch of salt and set the heat to a medium – bringing the water to a boil.

Then toss in your pasta and lower the temperature to medium-low. Let the pasta simmer for about 10 minutes.

In a separate bowl, whisk the vinegar, salt, pepper, oregano, and 3 tbsp of oil.

Once the pasta has softened, drain it through a colander.

Remove the roast vegetables from the oven, once cooked.

Mix the pasta, vegetables, crumbled feta, and vinegar mixture in a bowl and garnish with oregano.

APPLEBEE GREENS PASTA SALAD

Preparation Time: 15 minutes

Cooking Time: 25 minutes

Serving: 10

Ingredients:

1 lb. of short pasta

1 lb. of sliced cucumber

8 oz of crumbled feta cheese

1 tsp of salt

6 tbsp olive oil

2 tbsp of mustard

1 tsp of lemon zest

6 tbsps. of lemon juice

2 cloves of garlic, grated

½ tsp of black pepper

½ tsp of crushed chili

1 pack of cilantro leaves

½ cup of mint

Directions:

Fill a medium-sized pot halfway with water and add a pinch of salt. Bring the water to boil then add in your pasta. Cook for 10 minutes until al dente, then drain the pasta using a colander.

Place the pasta into a large/wide bowl and add 2 tbsps. of oil. Toss until the pasta is evenly coated.

In a separate bowl, whisk mustard, lemon zest, lemon juice, garlic, salt, pepper, 4 tbsp of oil, and crushed chili together. Add in the cucumbers and feta to the bowl and toss/gently stir with a big spoon until all the contents are well mixed.

Combine the pasta and then mix and give it one last mix. Garnish your pasta salad with cilantro and mint just before serving and you have the perfect summer pasta salad!

CHAPTER 4:

Soups and Side Dishes Recipes

RED LOBSTER GARLIC GREEN BEANS

Preparation Time: 20 minutes

Cooking Time: 30 minutes

Servings: 10

Ingredients:

800 g of fresh green beans

2 cloves of garlic

1 tablet of vegetable broth

1 teaspoon chopped thyme

1 lemon

2 tablespoons olive oil

Salt

Directions:

Cut the ends of the beans, remove the strands and chop them. Peel and crush the garlic cloves together with the thyme in a mortar. Put the oil in a pan and sauté the beans 3 or 4 minutes, add the mashed garlic and sauté 3 more minutes over low heat, without letting the garlic burn. Add water just to cover, pour the crumbled broth and salt to taste. Cook until the beans are tender (about 15-20 minutes), drain them, and water them with the lemon juice.

PANERA CREAMY TOMATO SOUP

Preparation Time: 10 minutes

Cooking Time: 15 minutes

Servings: 3

Ingredients:

2 tbsp. olive oil

1 cup white onions, chopped

2 tsp. garlic, minced

60 ounces' tomato puree

2 tsp. basil, dried

1/2 tsp. oregano

15 ounces' vegetable stock

1/2 cup cream

1 tsp. sugar

Salt to taste

Black pepper to taste

Directions:

In a saucepan, add olive oil and heat over medium heat and chopped white onion. Sprinkle of salt on top. Sauté until transparent to the onions. Add the chopped garlic and sauté until fragrant. Tomatoes puree, basil, vegetable stock, oregano, and heavy cream are added. Reduce to simmer oil. Simmer for 9-10 minutes. Nice taste, and apply sugar if the soup is too acid. You can make puree soup with either an electric mixer or in a blender. Season it with salt and black pepper.

Applebee's French Onion Soup

Preparation Time: 25 minutes

Cooking Time:1 hour 20 minutes

Servings: 8

Ingredients:

2 tbsp. butter

2 tbsp. vegetable oil

6 to 7 onions, sliced

1 tsp. salt

1 1/2 tsp. garlic, chopped

10 cups beef broth

1 tbsp. beef base

1 tsp. black pepper

8 slices bread

8 tsp. grated Parmesan cheese

8 tbsp. Provolone cheese

Directions:

Heat first the butter and oil in a large stockpot over medium heat, then add the sliced onions and salt; sauté the onions until browned. That will take up to half an hour; you want the caramel color of the onions. Frequently remove to prevent burning.

Add the chopped garlic when the Onions are almost caramelized to the full.

Cook the onion and garlic together for about 2 minutes, until the garlic has become fragrant. Add the broth, the base of the beef, and the black pepper. Taste, and if necessary, add more salt. Simmer over low heat for 30-45 minutes.

Preheat the oven to broil, to serve soup.

Ladle soup into 8 individual ovenproof cups, put a slice of bread on top of each, add 1 tsp. of Parmesan cheese to top each slice, and provolone cheese.

Put it under the broiler and cook until the cheese starts browning.

Take out in a bowl and enjoy your soup!

OLIVE GARDEN MINESTRONE SOUP

Preparation Time: 10 minutes

Cooking Time: 30 minutes

Servings: 4

Ingredients:

2 carrots, cut in cubes

2 zucchinis, cut in cubes

1 onion, chopped in cubes

6 celeries, cut in cubes

2 cloves garlic

30 ounces canned tomatoes, diced

3 ounces' vegetable broth

15 ounces canned Northern beans

15 ounces canned Kidney beans

3/4 tbsp. Italian seasoning

3/4 tbsp. dry basil

1/2 cup noodles

1 tbsp. olive oil

2 1/4 cups water

Directions:

Preheat the pot with olive oil, then add the carrots, celery, and carrots. Sauté the vegetables for about 10 minutes, until they soften.

Add canned tomatoes to the pot—season with dry basil and Italian seasoning.

A bowl of chicken broth and vegetables

Stir in vegetable broth, noodles, kidney, and beans from Great Northern. Simmer for 10 minutes, on. You can add more water to the mix according to the thickness of the soup.

Bread pot and pasta

Place the garlic in the mixture and allow it to cook for around 10 minutes.

Minestrone pot soup

Serve while warming up the minestrone.

OLIVE GARDEN ZUPPA TOSCANA SOUP

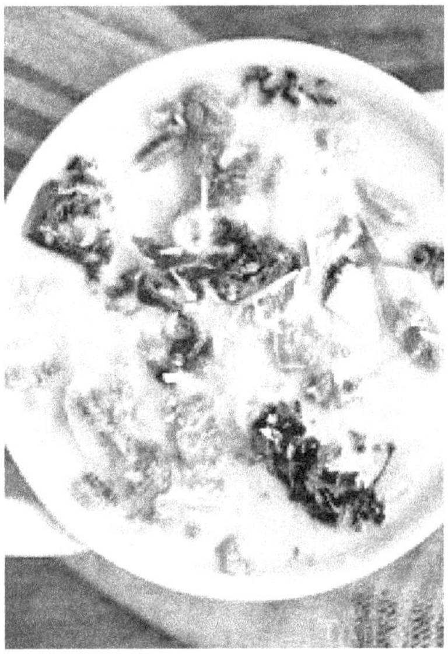

Preparation Time: 10 minutes

Cooking Time: 35 minutes

Servings: 2

Ingredients:

2 tsp. olive oil

1 lb. Italian Sausage

4 ounces' bacon, diced

1 cup yellow onion

3 cans of chicken broth

1 cup of water

1 1/2 lbs. potatoes, sliced into halves,

1 1/2 tsp. sugar

1/2 tsp. fennel seeds

Salt and black pepper to taste

1 1/2 cups half and half

1 1/2 cups chopped cabbage

Directions:

In a saucepan, heat the oil. Crumble the sausage and add to the pan.

Cook the sausage, sometimes stirring until cooked through. Drain the sausage onto a plate or baking platter lined with paper towels, set aside the sausage.

Attach the diced bacon to the saucepan, return to heat and sauté for 3 minutes, occasionally stirring.

Add the diced onions and sauté until the bacon is cooked and the onions are translucent for around 4-5 minutes.

To taste, add chicken broth, tea, sugar, sliced potatoes, fennel seeds, salt, and pepper. Bring the soup to a boil and then reduce to medium-low heat and whisk in cooked sausage.

Cover the saucepan and simmer, occasionally stirring, around 11-15 minutes, until the potatoes are almost tender.

Then add in the cabbage and simmer until the potatoes are soft.

Cut in half, and warm through. Use a spoon or ladle if you wish to remove excess fat from the top of the soup. Serve!

PEI WEI CHICKEN NOODLE SOUP

Preparation Time: 5 minutes

Cooking Time: 4 hours 15 minutes

Servings: 6

Ingredients:

2 boneless, skinless chicken breasts

1 cup egg noodles

2 cups water or as required

onion, small, diced

2 cans chicken broth

1 teaspoon thyme

2 cups celery, diced

1 bay leaf

2 cups carrots, diced

1 teaspoon minced garlic or garlic

Pepper and salt to taste

Directions:

Place the entire ingredients (except the egg noodles) in the bottom of your crockpot; give everything a good stir until evenly combined.

Cover & cook for 3 to 4 hours on high-heat or 6 to 8 hours on low heat.

Just 30 minutes before you serve this soup, remove the chicken pieces & shred.

Place them to the pot again. Turn on the high of your crockpot & add in the egg noodles; let cook for half an hour.

Serve immediately and enjoy it.

McDonald Brussels Sprout N' Kale Salad

Preparation Time: 5 minutes

Cooking Time: 1 minute

Servings: 6

Ingredients:

1 bunch kale

1-pound Brussels sprouts

¼ cup raisins (or dry cranberries)

½ cup pecans, chopped

Maple vinaigrette:

½ cup olive oil

¼ cup apple cider vinegar

¼ cup maple syrup

1 teaspoon dry mustard

Directions:

Slice the kale and Brussels sprouts with a cheese grater or mandolin slicer. Transfer to a salad bowl.

Add the pecans to a skillet on high heat. Toast for 60 seconds, then transfer to the salad bowl. Add the raisins. Mix all of the ingredients for the vinaigrette and whisk to combine. Pour the vinaigrette over the salad and toss. Refrigerate for a few hours or preferably overnight before serving.

Bob Evan's Hearty Beef Vegetable Soup

Preparation Time: 20 minutes

Cooking Time: 11 hours 10minutes

Servings: 5

Ingredients:

1-pound beef, lean ground

1 onion, chopped

1/2 tsp. salt

1/4 tsp. pepper

2 1/2 cups water

3 potatoes, and cut into cubes

1 can Italian diced tomatoes,

1 cup celery

1 cup carrots

2 tbsp. sugar

1 tbsp. dried parsley flakes

2 tsp. dried basil

1 bay leaf

Directions:

Cook onion and beef in a nonstick skillet over medium heat until meat is no longer pink, and split meat into crumbles; rinse.

Season with salt and pepper.

Shift Slow-cooking. Add ingredients left over.

Cover and simmer for 10-11 hours or until vegetables are soft.

Dispose of a bay leaf before serving.

Copycat Olive Garden's Creamy Zuppa Toscana

Preparation Time: 15 minutes

Cooking Time: 50 minutes

Servings: 4

Ingredients:

2 cups sweet yellow onion, quartered and sliced

½ cup sweet cream butter

½ teaspoon salt

1 tablespoon flour

4 cups beef stock

1 tablespoon fresh thyme

1 teaspoon coarse ground black pepper

4 baguette slices, approximately ½-inch thick

8 slices Provolone cheese

Directions:

Melt the butter in a stockpot over medium heat.

Add the onions and salt, and sauté for 3 minutes or until translucent but not browned.

Add the flour and stir.

Add the beef stock, increase the heat to medium-high, and bring to a boil.

Let boil for 1 minute.

Reduce the heat to low, season with thyme and black pepper.

Cover and let simmer for 25-30 minutes.

While the soup is simmering, toast the baguette slices to a medium golden brown.

Make sure each slice will fit comfortably in your soup bowl.

Preheat the broiler.

When the soup is done simmering, ladle it into ovenproof serving bowls.

Top each bowl with a toasted baguette slice and 2 slices of Provolone cheese.

Place under the broiler for 1-2 minutes, or until the cheese is well melted and lightly caramelized.

Remove from the broiler carefully and serve immediately

IHOP FRIJOLES NEGROS (CUBAN BLACK BEANS)

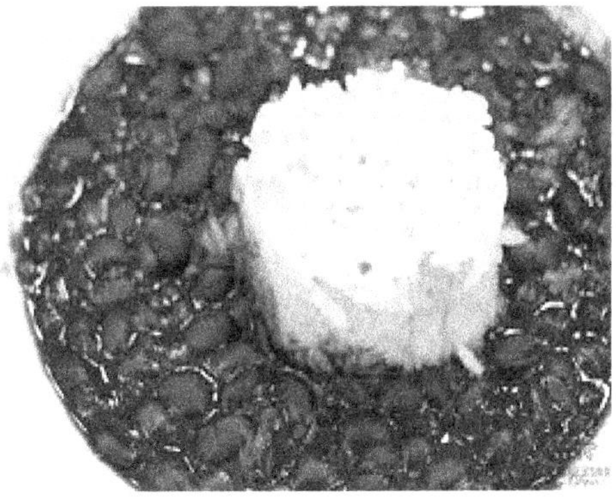

Preparation Time: 30 minutes

Cooking Time: 1 hour

Servings: 8

Ingredients:

450 grams of black beans

10 cups of Water (2400 milliliters)

6 tablespoons olive oil

1 unit large onion

5 cloves of garlic

¼ tablespoon oregano dessert

1 bay leaf

¼ tablespoon ground cumin dessert

1 pinch of salt

1 pinch of pepper

1 tablespoon vinegar

1 tablespoon dry wine

1 tablespoon of sugar

1 unit large green chili pepper

Directions:

To start with our recipe for Cuban beans, the first thing we are going to do is to wash the beans well and soak them with water and a bay leaf. Ideally, leave them overnight so that they inflate and you can cook them better.

The next day, take a pot with enough capacity, pour the beans in it with the water and the bay leaf and cook them for approximately 45 minutes until they are soft.

When they are ready, drain them and prepare the black bean stir fry. To do this, take a deep pan and heat the olive oil. Once hot, add the finely chopped onion and chili, or crushed if desired, and crushed garlic. Remove it with a wooden spoon and fry it.

Of the already soft beans, reserve a cup for later, the rest add it to the frypan, with the blade included. Remove everything, add salt and pepper to taste, oregano, cumin, and sugar and simmer for a few minutes. Do not stop stirring to prevent black beans from sticking and burning.

Then, mash the beans you reserved in the cup, add them to the rest and simmer them for half an hour and with the pan covered.

After the time, add the dry wine and the vinegar, stir it well and let it rest with the fire for at least 10 minutes. When they are ready to add two tablespoons of olive oil, integrate it and serve the black beans to the Cuban accompanied by white rice.

CHAPTER 5:

Fish Recipes

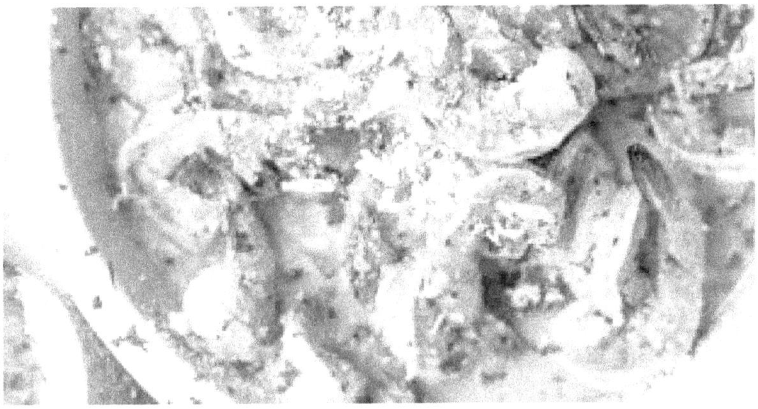

RED LOBSTER'S SHRIMP SCAMPI

Preparation time: 5 minutes

Cooking time: 10 minutes

Servings: 4

Ingredients:

1 ¼ pound shrimp, tail removed, peeled, deveined

1 ½ tablespoon minced garlic

2 scallions, sliced

¾ teaspoon salt

½ teaspoon ground black pepper

¼ teaspoon red pepper flakes

¼ cup chopped parsley

4 tablespoons butter, unsalted

¼ cup juice

¼ cup chardonnay

½ cup shredded Parmesan cheese

Directions:

Take an outsized skillet pan, place it over medium heat, add butter and when it melts, add garlic and cook for 1 minute until tender and golden brown.

Add shrimps, cook them for 3 to 4 minutes until bottom turns pink, then flip the shrimps by using tongs, sprinkle with red pepper flakes, and continue cooking for 3 minutes.

Then drizzle wine and juice over shrimps, cook another minute then remove the pan from heat.

Sprinkle scallions and parsley over the shrimps, season with salt and black pepper, then top with cheese.

Serve immediately.

RED LOBSTER CHEDDAR BAY BISCUITS

Preparation time: 10 minutes

Cooking time: 11 minutes

Servings: 9

Ingredients:

1 ½ cups almond flour

1 teaspoon garlic powder

¼ teaspoon salt

1 tablespoon leaven

½ cup shredded cheddar

½ cup soured cream

4 tablespoons butter, unsalted, melted

2 eggs

For the Topping:

½ teaspoon garlic powder

2 tablespoons butter, unsalted, melted

1 tablespoon minced parsley

Directions:

Switch on the oven, then set it to 450 degrees F and let it preheat.

Take an outsized bowl, place flour in it then stir in garlic, leaven, and salt until combined.

Take a little bowl, crack the eggs in it, whisk in butter and sour cream until smooth, then stir in almond flour mixture until smooth batter comes together.

Take a 12-cups muffin pan, grease the cups with oil, evenly fill them with batter then bake for 11 minutes until the highest of every biscuit turns golden brown and inserted toothpick into each biscuit comes out clean.

Meanwhile, take a little bowl, place melted butter in it, stir in garlic powder until dissolved then stir in parsley.

When done, remove biscuit from the pan, transfer them to a baking sheet then immediately brush the garlic-parsley butter on top of every biscuit.

Serve immediately.

PEI WEI FISH AND CHIPS

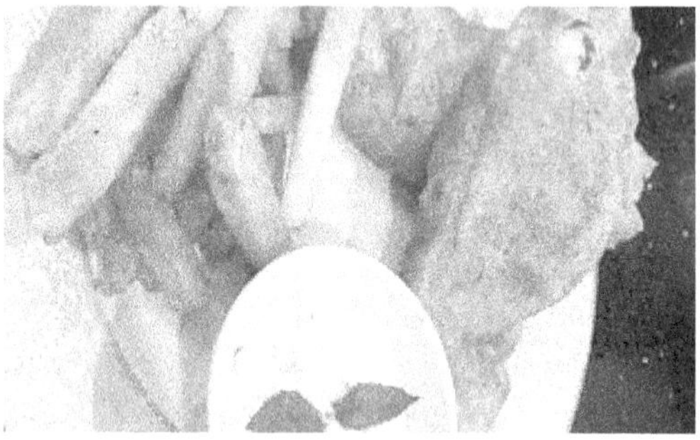

Preparation time: 15 minutes

Cooking time: 30 minutes

Servings: 2

Ingredients:

For the Chips:

1 medium zucchini

¼ teaspoon salt

¼ teaspoon ground black pepper

½ tablespoon avocado oil

For the fish:

¾ pound cod

½ cup almond flour

¼ teaspoon onion Powder

½ teaspoon salt

1/3 teaspoon ground black pepper

½ teaspoon paprika powder

4 cups avocado oil

1 egg

½ cup grated Parmesan cheese

For the Dipping Sauce:

¼ tablespoon flavored

2 tablespoons pickle relish

½ cup mayonnaise

Directions:

Prepare the dipping sauce and for this, take a medium bowl, place all of its ingredients in it, whisk until combined, and then put aside until required.

Switch on the oven, then set it to 400 degrees F and let it preheat.

Meanwhile, cut the zucchini into thin fries, place them during a medium bowl, drizzle with oil then toss until coated.

Spread the zucchini pieces on a baking sheet, season with salt and black pepper, then bake for a half-hour until golden brown, tossing halfway.

Meanwhile, prepare the fish and for this, crack the egg during a shallow dish then whisk until frothy.

Take a separate shallow dish, place flour in it, add all the spices and cheese, then stir until combined.

Cut the dish into a 1-by-1-inch piece, dredge each bit into the almond flour mixture, read egg, then dredge again with almond flour mixture.

Take an outsized skillet pan, place it over medium heat, add oil, let it heat for 12 minutes until it reaches 360 degrees F, then add prepared fish pieces and cook them for 4 minutes per side until golden brown and cooked.

Divide baked zucchini fries evenly between two plates, add fried fish then serve with the dipping sauce.

THE CHEESECAKE FACTORY'S TUNA TATAKI SALAD

Preparation time: 10 minutes

Cooking time: 5 minutes

Servings: 4

Ingredients:

For the Tuna:

1-pound tuna, sashimi grade

4 tablespoons avocado oil

For the Salad:

4 radishes, peeled, sliced thinly

8 cups salad greens

4 scallions, sliced

4 avocados, peeled, pitted, sliced

2 teaspoons black sesame seeds

For the Salad Dressing:

2 1-inch pieces of ginger, grated 2 tablespoons liquid stevia

4 tablespoons ponzu sauce, low-carb

2 tablespoons sake

2 tablespoons soy

2 tablespoons toasted vegetable oil

Directions:

Prepare the dressing and for this, take a Mason jar, place all of its ingredients in it, shut with the lid, then shake well until well blended, put aside until required.

Take an outsized salad bowl, place avocado slices, radish, and salad greens in it, then toss until mixed.

Prepare the tuna and for this, take an outsized skillet pan, place it over medium heat, add oil and when hot, add tuna then cook for 1 minute per side until seared.

Transfer tuna to a plate, repeat with the remaining tuna, let cool for a quarter-hour then cut tuna into thin slices.

Distribute salad evenly among four plates, add seared tuna to the side then drizzle with prepared dressing.

Sprinkle sesame seeds and scallion over tuna then serve.

Outback Steakhouse's Coconut Shrimp

Preparation time: 10 minutes

Cooking time: 14 minutes

Servings: 4

Ingredients:

1-pound medium shrimp, tail removed, peeled, deveined, and cooked

½ cup pork rind

1 teaspoon salt

½ cup shredded coconut, unsweetened

½ teaspoon ground black pepper

¼ cup coconut milk, unsweetened

Directions:

Take a shallow pan, place it over low heat and when hot, add coconut and cook for 3 to 4 minutes until golden brown.

Take a shallow dish, then pour within the milk.

Take a separate shallow dish, place coconut and pork rind in it, and then stir until mixed.

Pat dry the shrimp with paper towels, then dip each shrimp into milk and dredge within the pork-coconut mixture until evenly coated.

Plugin the air fryer, insert a greased fryer basket, set it 400 degrees F, and let it preheat for 400 degrees F.

Then add shrimps during a single layer into the fryer basket then fry for 7 minutes, shaking halfway.

When done, transfer fried shrimps to a plate and repeat with the remaining shrimps.

Add black pepper and salt to the shrimps then serve.

Red Lobster Tempura Fried Prawns

Preparation Time: 15 minutes

Cooking Time: 10 minutes

Serving: 10

Ingredients:

4 prawns (deveined & cleaned)

4 slices of sweet potato

2 slices of Renkon (alternatively, you can use other vegetables)

2 slices of shiso

50g of all-purpose flour

1 tbsp of mayonnaise

oil, for frying For homemade Tentsuyu dipping sauce (optional)

½ tbsp of Dashi powder

¼ cup of Mirin

¼ cup of Soy sauce

¼ cup of grated daikon

Directions:

Wash, cut, and clean your prawns and vegetables.

In a bowl, combine the flour with 2 ½ oz of water, and 1 tbsp of mayonnaise. Mix well and place in the refrigerator for later.

In a deep pan/skillet fill it to about ⅓ with oil and bring to medium-high heat.

Once the oil has heated up (little bubbles should form on the surface), take your flour batter out of the fridge and dip your vegetables and prawns into the batter, coating them well.

Fry the vegetables and prawns in the oil (make sure they do not touch each other), for about 3-5 minutes for each item.

The batter should turn a golden brown, this will indicate its readiness.

Place the contents on a paper towel to drain out the extra oil.

To make the dipping sauce: heat a small pan over the stove on high heat.

Pour in the mirin sauce and bring to boil for 1 minute. Stir in 1 cup of water, soy sauce, and dashi powder, bring the mixture to a boil.

Pour the sauce into a small bowl and allow it to cool down.

Garnish each serving of Tentsuyu dipping sauce with 1 tbsp of daikon and serve with Tempura.

McDonald Sushi

Preparation Time: 15 minutes

Cooking Time: 20 minutes + cooling time for the sushi rice

Serving: 10

Ingredients:

6 sheets of seaweed 1 1/2 cups of sushi rice

½ lb. of raw salmon/tuna, thinly sliced

4 oz of cream cheese

1 avocado, cut into thin slices

1 carrot, cut into short, thin slices

1 tbsp of mayonnaise

soy sauce, wasabi & ginger for serving

Directions:

Boil your sushi rice in ½ a pot of water for about 20 minutes. Drain the rice through a sieve and set it aside to cool down.

Prepare your working station: Layout the sliced avocado, sliced carrot, cream cheese, and sliced fish around the station. Get a glass of water ready and place a tablespoon in it.

Layout one sheet of seaweed, with the shinier side on the bottom. Using the wet tablespoon, smear sushi rice over ¾ of the seaweed sheet, leaving 1 inch of the seaweed bare. 1 inch into the rice, layer slices of fish, carrot, avocado, and a dollop of cream cheese. Roll the seaweed tightly and once you reach the end, wet your fingertips and pat it on the seaweed (so that it becomes sticky) and stick the seaweed to the roll, tightly closing it.

Using a sharp knife, cut the roll in half, then again, until it is in 8 equal small rolls.

Repeat the process until the contents are finished. Alternatively, you can make sashimi and/or nigiri with the remaining contents.

Place a dollop of mayonnaise on each sushi roll and serve with soy sauce, wasabi, and ginger.

Panera Seared Scallops with Coconut Lemongrass Sauce

Preparation Time: 10 minutes

Cooking Time: 15 minutes

Serving: 10

Ingredients:

1 lb. of scallops/shrimp

1 shallot, diced

1 tbsp of coconut oil

4 tbsps. of white vinegar

1 lime (zest & juice)

1 stalk of lemongrass, smashed

2 slices of ginger

1 can of coconut milk

1 ½ types of fish sauce

½ tsp of chili flakes/1 red chili chopped finely

salt and pepper to taste

a handful of basil leaves, chopped thinly

rice/couscous for meal serving

sriracha sauce (optional)

Directions:

Set the rice/couscous to cook while you prep the rest of the meal. Heat the vinegar in a small pan and toss in the shallots, leave on low heat for 5 minutes, until the vinegar reduces. Pour in the coconut milk, ½ of the lime zest, lemongrass, and ginger. Stir to combine the flavors and leave to simmer for 5 minutes. Next, pour in the fish sauce, 1 tbsp of lime juice, and chili flakes. Remove the mixture from heat and set aside. Wash and pat dry your scallops/shrimp (make sure you've cleaned and deveined them too). Season the scallops with salt and pepper.

Heat a skillet with coconut oil over medium heat and then place the scallops in, searing them for 2-3 minutes on either side.

Serve the scallops with couscous/rice and drizzle the sauce over, alternatively you can enjoy the scallops & sauce alone. Garnish with basil, lime zest, and a drop of sriracha for the extra spicy kick!

IHOP Bang Bang Shrimp

Preparation time: 10 minutes

Cooking time: 12 minutes

Servings: 4

Ingredients:

For the Shrimp:

1-pound shrimp, tail removed, peeled, deveined ½ cup coconut flour

Avocado oil as required for frying

1 scallion, sliced

For the Sauce:

1/3 cup mayonnaise

1 ¾ tablespoon garlic condiment

1 ½ tablespoon rice vinegar

2 ½ tablespoons monk fruit Sweetener

1/8 teaspoon salt

Directions:

Prepare the shrimps and for this, dredge each shrimp in coconut flour then arrange on a baking sheet.

Then take an outsized skillet pan, place it over medium-high heat, fill it 2-inch with oil and when hot, add shrimps in it then cook for 4 minutes or more until pink.

When done, transfer shrimps to a plate lined with paper towels and repeat with the remaining shrimps.

Prepare the sauce and for this, connect a kitchen appliance, add all the ingredients in it, cover with the lid, then pulse for 30 seconds until smooth.

Tip the sauce into an outsized bowl, add shrimps then toss until coated.

Garnish shrimps with scallion then serve.

TGI Friday Fish Cakes

Preparation time: 5 minutes

Cooking time: 16 minutes

Servings: 2

Ingredients:

For the Fish Cake:

1-pound white fish, boneless

¼ cup cilantro leaves

¼ teaspoon salt

¼ teaspoon red chili flakes

1 tablespoon minced garlic

2 tablespoons avocado oil

For the Dip:

1 lemon, juiced

2 avocados, peeled, pitted

¼ teaspoon salt

2 tablespoons water

Directions:

Prepare the fish cakes and for this, place all of its ingredients during a kitchen appliance apart from oil then pulse for 3 minutes until well combined.

Tip the mixture during a large bowl then shape it into six patties.

Take a frypan, place it over medium-high heat, add oil and when hot, add fish patties in it then cook for 3 to 4 minutes per side until cooked and golden brown.

Meanwhile, prepare the dip and for this, place all of its ingredients during a kitchen appliance then pulse for two minutes until smooth.

Serve fish cakes with prepared dip.

CHAPTER 6:

Beef and Pork Recipes

PANDA EXPRESS PAN-COOKED STEAK

Preparation Time: 5 minutes

Cooking Time: 10 minutes

Serving: 10

Ingredients:

2 ribeye steaks (about 1 inch thick)

1 tsp of salt

3 tbsps. of unsalted butter

3 smashed cloves of garlic (or 1 ½ tbsps. of garlic paste)

3 rosemary/thyme sprigs

Directions:

Remove the steaks from the refrigerator at least 1 hour before cooking. Pat the steaks dry with a paper towel.

Lightly coat the steaks with salt – making sure both sides are well seasoned.

Place a large cast-iron pan over high heat and allow to preheat for about 10 minutes. Place the steaks in the pan and leave to cook for 1 minute, then flip. Leave to cook for 1 more minute then flip again. Do this for up to 4 minutes, flipping 4 times.

Pour in the butter, garlic, and rosemary into the pan and use a spoon to baste the seasoned, melted butter over the steak. Flip the steak and baste again. Repeat this process for about 6 minutes, until the steak is medium-rare.

Plate the steaks and allow them to rest for 5 minutes then transfer over to a cutting board and thinly slice the meat. Drizzle pan juice over the meat and serve immediately.

CHILI FROM STEAK N' SHAKE

Preparation Time: 20 minutes

Cooking Time: 6 minutes

Servings: 6

Ingredients:

1 tablespoon olive oil

2 pounds ground beef

½ teaspoon salt

2 tablespoons onion powder

1 tablespoon chili powder

2 teaspoons ground cumin

½ teaspoon ground black pepper

2 teaspoons cocoa powder

6 ounces canned tomato paste

13½ ounces canned tomato sauce

1 cup Pepsi

27 ounces canned kidney beans, rinsed and drained

Shredded cheese, sliced green onions for toppings, if desired

Directions:

Heat oil in a pan. Add beef and cook until brown, drain, then remove from heat.

In a bowl, add cooked meat, salt, onion powder, chili powder, cumin, pepper, cocoa powder, tomato paste, tomato sauce, and Pepsi. Mix until combined.

Pour mixture into a blender and puree until well blended.

Add mixture into a slow cooker. Pour in beans. Cover and set the slow cooker to the low setting and cook for 6 hours.

Serve with shredded cheese and green onions, if desired, on top.

SMOKEHOUSE PORK BELLY SANDWICH FROM ARBY'S

Preparation Time: 15 minutes

Cooking Time: 2 hours and 30 minutes

Servings: 6

Ingredients:

2 pounds center-cut pork belly

Salt and pepper, to taste

1-2 tablespoons barbecue spice rub

6-star cross buns

Cooking spray

½ pound smoked cheddar cheese

½ cup mayonnaise

½ cup any smoky barbecue sauce

6 ounces onion strings

Directions:

Sprinkle salt and pepper onto pork belly then coat with barbecue rub. Set smoker to 300°F with hickory wood on coals. Put pork belly in a smoker with the flat side facing down. Smoke for about 2½ hours until well browned and a bit charred. Pork is ready once its internal temperature is about 185 to 195°F. Spray cooking spray onto the inner sides of buns then toast until golden brown.

Assemble sandwich by layering mayo, cooked pork belly, barbecue sauce, cheese, and onion strings on the bottom bun. Top with the second bun. Repeat for remaining sandwiches.

Serve.

TACO BELL BEEF STROGANOFF

Preparation Time: 10 minutes

Cooking Time: 35 minutes

Serving: 10

Ingredients

3 tbsps. of butter, divided

8 oz of mushrooms, thinly sliced

1 onion, diced

2 cloves of garlic, finely chopped

1 lb. of ground beef

3 tbsps. of all-purpose flour

1 ¼ tsps. of paprika

4 cups of beef broth

1 tbsp of Dijon mustard

8 oz of dried egg noodles

¾ cup of Greek yogurt

salt and pepper to taste

1 tbsp of parsley leaves

Directions:

In a large, deep-set pot, melt 1 tbsp of butter over medium-high heat. Stir in the mushrooms and sprinkle salt and pepper to taste. Fry the mushrooms for about 5 minutes, until brown, stirring regularly. Set the mushrooms aside. Lower the heat to medium and mix 2 more tbsps. of butter into the pot. Mix in the onions, garlic, salt, and pepper to taste and stir until the onions have softened – about 5 minutes. Add in the beef into the pot and mix with the onions and spices, breaking the meat apart as you stir. Cook until the meat has browned.

Mix in the paprika and flour, stir for another 2 minutes then add in the broth and mustard and mix well. Bring the pot to a medium-high and then lower to a simmer.

Bring the mushrooms back into the pot and stir for an additional 3-4 more minutes.

Remove from heat and stir the yogurt in. Season again with salt and pepper and garnish with parsley.

Serve with your desired carbs, such as pasta, mashed potatoes, or rice.

CHILI GLAZED STICKY PORK

Preparation Time: 15 minutes

Cooking Time: 10 minutes

Serving: 10

Ingredients:

1 ½ lbs. of pork loin, cut into 3 inch long strips

1 tsp of salt

½ tsp of pepper

1 tbsp of oil

3 tbsps. of garlic paste

2 inches of ginger, grated

4 tbsps. of sriracha sauce (or more, if you'd like it extra spicy)

½ cup of honey

1 tbsp of white wine vinegar

Directions:

In a small bowl, whisk the honey, sriracha, and white wine vinegar together until well mixed, then set aside.

Season the pork strips with salt and pepper and toss to fully, evenly coat them.

Heat a medium pan over medium-high heat and drizzle the oil to lightly coat the pan. Bring to a simmer and then place in the pork strips – do this in batches so that the strips do not touch one another. Once browned, flip the strips over and fry the other side; it should take 2-3 minutes on either side.

Set the pork strips aside and pour the garlic and ginger into the pan, stirring for about 30 seconds. Raise to high heat and pour the honey mixture into the pan, stirring well to combine. When the sauce begins to boil and thicken, stir the pork strips back into the pan and mix well to evenly coat the strips.

You can serve hot or cold.

P.F. CHANG BARBECUE PORK RIBS

Preparation Time: 15 minutes

Cooking Time: 2 hours 15 minutes

Serving: 10

Ingredients:

4 lbs. of pork ribs (2 racks)

¾ cup of apple cider

1 tbsp of olive oil Barbecue rub:

3 tsps. of paprika

2 tsps. of garlic powder

1 ½ tsps. of onion powder

1 tsp of cayenne pepper

1 ½ tsps. of thyme

1 ½ of oregano

1 ½ tsp of salt

½ tsp of pepper Barbecue sauce:

1 tsp of salt

1 tsp of pepper

½ cup of apple cider vinegar

1 ½ cups of ketchup

cup of water

1 ½ tbsp molasses

⅓ cup of brown sugar

2 tsps. of mustard powder

½ tsp of garlic powder

2 tsps. of Worcestershire sauce

1 tsps. of Tabasco

Directions:

In a small bowl, mix all of the ingredients for the barbecue rub and massage well into the pork ribs. Set aside to marinate for at least 20 minutes.

When ready to cook, preheat your oven to 350ºF and prepare a baking tray. Layer all of the ribs onto the tray and drizzle them with apple cider vinegar (coat underneath the ribs too). Cover the tray with foil and place in the oven for 1 hour and 30 minutes.

While the ribs are baking, mix the barbecue sauce in a bowl and set aside.

Closer to when the ribs are done, prepare another baking tray by lining with foil and then a layer of parchment paper over. Remove the ribs from the oven and place on the new tray, generously pouring the leftover juices from the tray over the ribs, coating well.

Flip the ribs over so that the boney sides are faced up, and baste the ribs in ¼ of the barbecue sauce. Place back in the oven for another 10 minutes.

Remove the ribs from the oven, flip them over and baste in another ¼ of sauce. Bake for another 5 minutes. Repeat this process, baking 5 minutes on each side, until the sauce is finished.

Slice the ribs into portions and serve!

TEXAS ROADHOUSE STUFFED CABBAGE ROLLS

Preparation Time: 15 minutes

Cooking Time: 45 minutes

Serving: 10

Ingredients:

For the cabbage & sauce:

1 cabbage head

1 tbsp of olive oil

1 onion, diced

tsps. of salt

¼ black pepper

1 can of tomatoes & the tomato juice

2 tbsps. of apple cider vinegar

¼ cup of raisins

3 tbsps. of brown sugar For the cabbage filling:

⅓ cup of uncooked rice

1 large egg

1 lb. of ground beef

¼ cup of diced onion

½ tbsp of garlic paste

2 tsps. of salt

1 tsp of paprika

¼ tsp of black pepper

Directions:

Bring a large pot of water to boil and wash the cabbage. Cut the cabbage in half; remove about 10-12 outer leaves. Place the leaves in the water and boil for about 2 minutes until wilted. Scoop the leaves out using a fork and place on a paper towel to drain.

In a large, deep-set pan, heat the oil over medium heat until simmering. Place in the onions and stir for 5 minutes until softened. Then pour in the tomatoes, vinegar, raisins, sugar, salt, and pepper and stir well. Leave to simmer for 15 minutes; prepare the cabbage filling in the meanwhile.

Combine all the filling ingredients except for the beef, in a bowl, and stir well. Slowly stir the beef, and then divide into 8 equal parts. Roll the portions into balls and place the meatballs into the centers of cabbage leaves and then wrap the cabbage around the balls, completely covering the meat mix. Use 2 leaves for meatballs if needed.

On a baking sheet, place the cabbage balls with their folds facing down. When the sauce is ready, place the cabbage balls into the pan with their seam-sides facing downwards. Spoon the sauce over the balls to cover them well. Cover the pot and leave to simmer for 35-40 minutes, until the rice filling is cooked.

P.F. Chang's Mongolian Beef

Preparation Time: 10 minutes

Cooking Time: 20 minutes

Servings: 2

Ingredients:

1 pound flank steak

¼ cup cornstarch

2 teaspoons

½ teaspoon ginger, finely chopped

1 tablespoon ginger, diced

½ soy sauce

½ cup water

½ cup brown sugar

1 cup vegetable oil, divided

6 green onions, cut diagonally into 2-inch pieces

Directions:

Cut steak against the grain into small pieces, about ¼ inch. Transfer steak into a bowl with cornstarch and flip until fully coated on all sides. Set aside. In a skillet, heat 1 tablespoon of the oil on medium heat. Stir in ginger and garlic. Cook for about 1 minute or until aromatic. Mix in soy sauce, water, and brown sugar. Keep stirring until sugar is melted. Bring to a boil on medium heat. Simmer for about 2 minutes or until sauce is thick. Heat remaining vegetable oil in a separate saucepan on medium heat until oil reaches 350°F. Deep-fry steak in batches for 2 minutes or until brown. Transfer onto a plate lined with paper towels. Discard the oil, then add sauce and stir in meat with sauce in a saucepan for about 2 minutes on medium heat. Mix in green onions and cook for an additional 1-2 minutes. Place meat and onions on a plate. Serve hot.

PANDA EXPRESS' BEIJING BEEF

Preparation Time: 30 minutes

Cooking Time: 15 minutes

Servings: 4

Ingredients: 1 egg

¼ teaspoon salt

6 tablespoons water

9 tablespoons cornstarch

1 pound flank steak

4 tablespoons sugar

3 tablespoons ketchup

2 tablespoons vinegar

¼ teaspoon chili pepper, crushed

1 cup vegetable oil

1 teaspoon garlic, finely chopped

1 red bell pepper, chopped

1 green bell pepper, chopped

1 white onion, chopped

Directions:

To make the marinade, add egg, salt, 2 tablespoons water, and 1 tablespoon cornstarch in a bowl. Mix well.

Slice steak against the grain into small strips. Transfer into a Ziploc bag and pour marinade inside. Seal tightly. Shake the bag gently to make sure the meat is well-coated. Set aside for at least 15 minutes.

To make the sauce, combine sugar, ketchup, vinegar, chili pepper, remaining 4 tablespoons water, and 2 teaspoons cornstarch in a bowl. Mix well. Cover and keep refrigerated.

Heat oil in a saucepan. Ready a bowl with 6 tablespoons cornstarch. Place beef in a bowl and toss until fully coated. Shake off excess cornstarch and cook beef in hot oil until golden brown. Transfer onto a plate lined with paper towels.

Remove excess oil from saucepan. Toss in the garlic, bell peppers, and onions and cook for about 2 minutes, stirring continuously. Transfer vegetables onto a plate.

In the same saucepan, add sauce and bring to a boil. Reduce heat to low and let simmer for 10 minutes.

Serve beef and vegetables with the sauce poured on top.

Edo Japan's Sukiyaki Beef

Preparation Time: 15 minutes

Cooking Time: 5 to 6 minutes

Marinating Time: 20 minutes

Servings: 2 to 4

Ingredients:

10 ounces sirloin steak, thinly sliced

½ carrot, thinly sliced

½ onion, sliced

1 green pepper, sliced

½ yellow bell pepper, sliced

½ cup sukiyaki sauce, divided

1 tablespoon oil

1 teaspoon chopped garlic

2 tablespoons ginger, finely chopped

2 teaspoons soy sauce

1 teaspoon sugar

1 tablespoon oyster sauce

Directions:

Pour half of the sukiyaki sauce into a medium bowl and add the sliced beef. Let the beef marinate for 20 minutes.

Heat the oil in a large skillet. Add the garlic and cook for about 30 seconds.

Add the beef, with the sauce. Cook over medium-high heat until the beef is cooked through.

Add the ginger, carrots, peppers, and onions and cook until the veggies have begun to soften.

Add the rest of the sukiyaki sauce along with the oyster sauce, soy sauce, and sugar. Cook and stir for about 2 more minutes.

Serve over rice.

CHAPTER 7:

Chicken Recipes

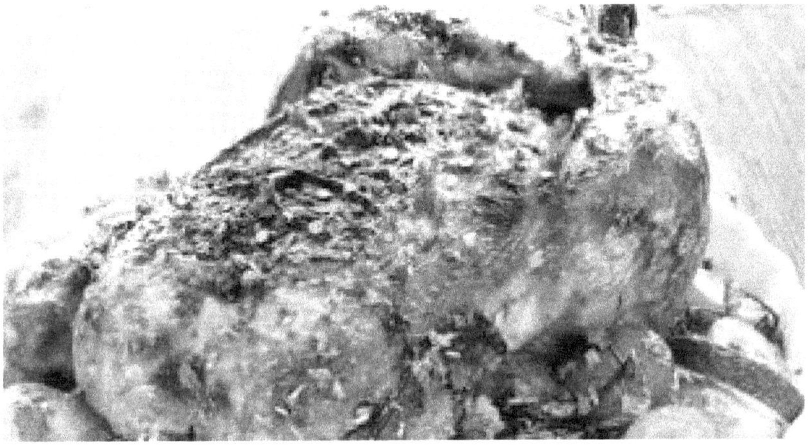

CHIPOTLE SUNDAY CHICKEN

Preparation Time: 10 minutes

Cooking Time: 10 minutes

Servings: 4

Ingredients:

Oil for frying

4 boneless, skinless chicken breasts

1 cups all-purpose flour

1 cup bread crumbs

2 teaspoons salt - 2 teaspoons black pepper

1 cup buttermilk

½ cup water

Directions:

Add 3–4 inches of oil to a large pot or a deep fryer and preheat to 350°F.

Mix the flour, breadcrumbs, salt, and pepper in a shallow dish. To a separate shallow dish, add the buttermilk and water; stir.

Pound the chicken breasts to a consistent size. Dry them with a paper towel, then sprinkle with salt and pepper.

Dip the seasoned breasts in the flour mixture, then the buttermilk mixture, then back into the flour.

Add the breaded chicken to the hot oil and fry for about 8 minutes. Turn the chicken as necessary so that it cooks evenly on both sides.

Remove the chicken to either a wire rack or a plate lined with paper towels to drain.

Serve with mashed potatoes or whatever sides you love.

Olive Garden Creamy Chicken and Rice

Preparation Time: 10 minutes

Cooking Time: 45 minutes

Servings: 4

Ingredients:

Salt and pepper to taste

2 cups cooked rice

1 diced onion

1 can cream of mushroom soup

1 packet chicken gravy

1½ pounds chicken breasts, cut into strips

Directions:

Preheat the oven to 350°F. Cook the rice. When it is just about finished, toss in the diced onion so that it cooks too. Prepare a baking dish by greasing or spraying with nonstick cooking spray. Dump the rice into the prepared baking dish. Layer the chicken strips on top. Spread the undiluted cream of mushroom soup over the chicken. In a small bowl, whisk together the chicken gravy with 1 cup of water, making sure to get all the lumps out. Pour this over the top of the casserole. Cover with foil and transfer to the oven. Bake for 45 minutes or until the chicken is completely cooked.

Alice Springs Chicken from Outback

Preparation Time: 5 minutes

Cooking Time: 2 hours and 30 minutes

Servings: 4

Ingredients:

Sauce:

½ cup Dijon mustard

½ cup honey

¼ cup mayonnaise

1 teaspoon fresh lemon juice

Chicken preparation:

4 chicken breast, boneless and skinless

2 tablespoons butter

1 tablespoon olive oil

8 ounces fresh mushrooms, sliced

4 slices bacon, cooked and cut into 2-inch pieces

2 ½ cups Monterrey Jack cheese, shredded

Parsley for serving (optional)

Directions:

Preheat oven to 400 °F.

Mix ingredients for the sauce in a bowl.

Put the chicken in a Ziploc bag, then add the sauce into the bag until only ¼ cup is left. Keep the remaining sauce in a container, cover, and refrigerate. Make sure to seal the Ziploc bag tightly and shake gently until chicken is coated with sauce Keep in the refrigerator for at least 2 hours.

Melt butter in a pan over medium heat. Toss in mushrooms and cook for 5 minutes or until brown. Remove from pan and place on a plate.

In an oven-safe pan, heat oil. Place marinated chicken flat in the pan and cook for 5 minutes on each side or until both sides turn golden brown.

Panda Express' Orange Chicken

Preparation Time: 15 minutes

Cooking Time: 30 minutes

Servings: 6

Ingredients:

Orange sauce:

1½ tablespoon soy sauce

1½ tablespoon water

5 tablespoons sugar

5 tablespoons white vinegar

3 tablespoons orange zest

Chicken preparation:

1 egg

1½ teaspoon salt

White pepper, to taste

5 tablespoons grapeseed oil, divided

½ cup + 1 tablespoon cornstarch

¼ cup flour

¼ cup cold water

2 pounds chicken breast, boneless and skinless, chopped

1 teaspoon fresh ginger, grated

1 teaspoon garlic, finely chopped

½ teaspoon hot red chili pepper, ground

¼ cup green onion, sliced 1 tablespoon rice wine

½ teaspoon sesame oil

White rice and steamed broccoli for serving

Directions:

Mix ingredients for the orange sauce in a bowl. Reserve for later.

Add egg, salt, pepper, and 1 tablespoon oil to a separate bowl. Mix well.

In another bowl, combine ½ cup cornstarch and flour. Mix until fully blended.

Add remaining cornstarch and cold water in a different bowl. Blend until cornstarch is completely dissolved.

Heat 3 tablespoons oil in a large deep skillet or wok over high heat.

Coat chicken pieces in the egg mixture. Let excess drip off. Then, coat in cornstarch mixture. Cook for at least 3 minutes or until both sides are golden brown and chicken is cooked through. Arrange on a plate lined with paper towels to drain excess oil.

In a clean large deep skillet, or wok heat remaining oil on high heat. Lightly sauté ginger and garlic for 30 seconds or until aromatic. Toss in peppers and green onions. Stir-fry vegetables for 1-3 minutes, then pour in rice wine. Mix well before adding the orange sauce. Bring to a boil. Mix in cooked chicken pieces, then adds cornstarch mixture. Simmer until mixture is thick, then mix in sesame oil. Transfer onto a plate and serve with white rice and steamed broccoli.

CRACKER BARREL CHICKEN POT PIE

Preparation Time: 30 minutes

Cooking Time: 30 minutes

Servings: 6 to 8

Ingredients:

½ cup butter

1 medium onion, diced

1 (14.5-ounce) can chicken broth

1 cup half and half milk

½ cup all-purpose flour

1 carrot, diced

1 celery stalk, diced

3 medium potatoes, peeled and diced

3 cups cooked chicken, diced

½ cup frozen peas

1 teaspoon chicken seasoning

½ teaspoon salt

½ teaspoon ground pepper

1 single refrigerated pie crust

1 egg

Water

Directions:

Preheat the oven to 375°F.

In a large skillet, heat the butter over medium heat, add the leeks and sauté for 3 minutes.

Sprinkle flour over the mixture, and continue to stir constantly for 3 minutes.

Whisking constantly, blend in the chicken broth and milk. Bring the mixture to a boil. Reduce heat to medium-low.

Add the carrots, celery, potatoes, salt, pepper, and stir to combine. Cook for 10-15 minutes or until veggies is cooked through but still crisp. Add chicken and peas. Stir to combine.

Transfer chicken filling to a deep 9-inch pie dish. Fit the pie crust sheet on top and press the edges around the dish to seal the crust. Trim the excess if needed.

In a separate bowl, whisk an egg with 1 tablespoon of water, and brush the mixture over the top of the pie. With a knife, cut a few slits to let steam escape.

Bake the pie in the oven on the middle oven rack 20 to 30 minutes until the crust becomes golden brown.

Let the pie rest for about 15 minutes before serving.

APPLEBEE GRILLED CHICKEN TENDERLOIN

Preparation Time: 10 minutes

Marinating Time: 1 hour

Cooking Time: 30 min

Servings: 4 to 5

Ingredients:

4–5 boneless and skinless chicken breasts, cut into strips, or 12 chicken tenderloins, tendons removed

1 cup Italian dressing

2 teaspoons lime juice

4 teaspoons honey

Directions:

Combine the dressing, lime juice, and honey in a plastic bag. Seal and shake to combine.

Place the chicken in the bag. Seal and shake again, then transfer to the refrigerator for at least 1 hour. The longer it marinates, the more the flavors will infuse into the chicken.

When ready to prepare, transfer the chicken and the marinade to a large nonstick skillet.

Bring to a boil, then reduce the heat and allow simmering until the liquid has cooked down to a glaze.

CHILI'S BONELESS BUFFALO WINGS

Preparation Time: 30 minutes

Cooking Time: 15 minutes

Servings: 2

Ingredients:

1 cup flour

2 teaspoons salt

½ teaspoon black pepper, ground

¼ teaspoon cayenne pepper, ground

1 egg

1 cup milk

5 cups vegetable oil

2 chicken breasts, boneless and skinless, cut into 6 pieces

¼ cup hot sauce

1 tablespoon margarine

1 blue cheese salad dressing

1 stalk celery, cut into sticks

Directions:

In a bowl, mix flour, salt, peppers, and paprika.

Add egg and milk to a separate bowl and mix well.

Preheat 5 cups oil in a deep-fryer to 375 °F.

Coat chicken pieces into the egg mixture. Allow excess to drip off, then coat with flour mixture. Repeat twice for a double coat.

Transfer breaded chicken onto a plate and refrigerate for about 15 minutes.

Deep-fry each for about 5 minutes or until brown and transfer onto a paper towel-lined plate.

Meanwhile, mix hot sauce and margarine in a bowl. Then, heat in the microwave for about 20 seconds or until melted. Mix well until fully blended.

Place chicken pieces in a large Ziploc bag and add the sauce. Seal bag tightly. Using your hands, mix chicken and sauce until well-coated.

Serve chicken pieces on a plate with blue cheese dressing and celery sticks on the side.

Boston Market's Rotisserie Chicken Copycat

Preparation Time: 24 hours

Cooking Time: 1 hour

Servings: 4

Ingredients:

¼ cup apple cider vinegar

½ cup canola oil

2 tablespoons brown sugar

4 fresh garlic cloves, finely chopped

1 whole roasting chicken

Directions:

Combine vinegar, oil, sugar, and garlic in a bowl. Add chicken and spoon mixture on top to coat well. Refrigerate overnight, making sure to turn chicken over to soak opposite side Remove chicken from refrigerator. Set aside for at least 20 minutes.

Bake at 350°F for about 45-50 minutes or until the temperature reads 165°F on an instant meat thermometer inserted in the thickest part of the thigh without touching any bones.

Serve.

CRACKER BARREL CHICKEN AND DUMPLINGS

Preparation Time: 1 hour

Cooking Time: 2 hours

Servings: 6

Ingredients:

1 whole chicken

2 quarts water

2 teaspoons salt

½ teaspoon pepper

2 cups all-purpose flour

½ teaspoon baking soda

½ teaspoon salt

3 tablespoons shortening

¾ cup buttermilk

Directions:

In a heavy-bottomed pot, boil the chicken in water mixed with salt. Cover, then lower heat. Simmer for about 1 hour or until tender enough that the meat almost falls off the bone.

Using a slotted spoon, transfer chicken to a plate and cool. Then, remove bones and chop into small pieces.

In the same pot, add broth and bring to a boil Add pepper.

In a bowl, mix flour, baking soda, and salt. Fold in shortening. Pour in buttermilk and mix everything until incorporated.

Knead dough 4 to 5 times. Pinch off about ½ inch size balls of dough and to the boiling broth. Reduce heat to medium-low. Simmer for about 8 to 10 minutes while stirring now and then.

Add chicken to pot and stir.

Serve immediately.

CHIPOTLE'S CHICKEN

Preparation Time: 10 minutes

Cooking Time: 20 minutes

Marinate Time: 24 hours

Servings: 8

Ingredients:

2 ½ pound organic boneless and skinless chicken breasts or thighs

Olive oil or cooking spray

Marinade

7 oz. chipotle peppers in adobo sauce

2 tablespoons olive oil

6 garlic cloves, peeled

1 teaspoon black pepper

2 teaspoons salt

½ teaspoon cumin

½ teaspoon dry oregano

Directions:

Pour all the marinade ingredients in a food processor or blender and blend until you get a smooth paste.

Pound the chicken until it has a thickness between ½ to ¾ inch. Place chicken into an airtight container or resealable plastic bag such as a Ziploc. Pour the marinade over the chicken and stir until well coated. Place the chicken in the refrigerator and let marinate overnight or up to 24 hours.

Pour the blended mixture into the container and marinate the chicken for at least 8 hours.

Cook the chicken over medium to high heat on an oiled and preheated grill for 3 to 5 minutes per side. The internal temperature of the chicken should be 165°F before you remove it from the heat. You can also cook it in a heavy-bottomed skillet over medium heat with a little olive oil.

Let rest before serving. If desired, cut into cubes to add to salads, tacos, or quesadillas or serve as is.

CHAPTER 8:

Burger and Sandwich Recipes

RED LOBSTER CHICK-FIL-A SANDWICH

Preparation Time: 10 minutes

Cooking Time: 20 minutes

Servings: 8

Ingredients:

Hamburger buns (4

split)

Lettuce (1 head)

Dill pickle (20 slices)

Sliced tomato (1)

Chicken breasts (2)

Milk

divided (1.5 cups)

Dill pickle juice (1 cup)

Egg (1 large)

All-purpose flour (.5 cup)

Kosher salt and freshly cracked black pepper (as desired)

Confectioners' sugar (1 tbsp.)

Peanut oil (1 cup)

Directions:

Slice the breast of chicken in half

horizontally on a cutting board, trimming away the fat.

Whisk the pickle juice and ½ cup milk. Toss in the chicken and marinate it for about 30 minutes. Drain well.

Prepare a skillet using the medium temperature setting to warm the oil.

Prepare another container and whisk egg and last cup of milk. Fold in the chicken to coat.

In a gallon-sized zipper-type bag, combine the flour, salt, pepper, and confectioners' sugar. Toss in the chicken and shake to cover.

Arrange the chicken in the skillet and fry for four to five minutes. (Prepare in batches if needed and drain on paper towels.)

Serve the chicken promptly on buns with lettuce, pickles, and tomatoes.

Pei Wei Sandwich

Preparation Time: 10 minutes

Cooking Time: 20 minutes

Servings: 8

Ingredients:

Large onion (1)

Country-style boneless pork ribs (2 lb.)

Ketchup (.5 cup)

Plum sauce (.25 cup)

Chili sauce (.25 cup)

Garlic powder (1 tsp.)

Brown sugar (2 tbsp.)

Celery seed (1 tsp.)

Optional: Liquid smoke (1 tsp.)

Ground allspice (.5 tsp.)

Split kaiser rolls (8)

Also Needed: 3-qt. slow cooker

Directions:

Chop and toss the onion into the cooker. Top with ribs. Combine the plum sauce, ketchup, brown sugar, chili sauce, garlic powder, celery seed, allspice, and liquid smoke -if desired and pour it over ribs.

Securely close the lid and set the timer for six to seven hours using the low-temperature setting. It should be tender.

Shred the meat by hand or with two forks. Serve the delicious meat on rolls and enjoy them in your "own" kitchen.

Egg Salad Sandwich

Preparation Time: 10 minutes

Cooking Time: 60 minutes

Servings: 8

Ingredients:

Hard-boiled eggs (8 large)

Unchilled cream cheese (3 oz.)

Mayonnaise (.25 cup)

Pepper (1/8 tsp.)

Salt (.5 tsp.)

Red/green sweet pepper (.25 cup)

Celery (.25 cup)

Fresh parsley (2 tbsp.)

Sweet pickle relish (.25 cup)

Directions:

Combine the mayo, salt, pepper, and cream cheese until it's creamy smooth.

Finely chop and add the celery, green pepper, parsley, and relish.

Chop and fold in the eggs.

Cover and chill before serving.

McDonald Sausage Cheddar & Egg Breakfast Sandwich

Preparation Time: 10 minutes

Cooking Time: 30 minutes

Servings: 8

Ingredients:

Crumbled blue cheese (4 oz./1 cup)

Jalapeno (1 pepper seeded)

Dry Seasonings

1 tsp. of each:

Parsley flakes

Oregano

Dried basil

Bulk Italian sausage (1 lb.)

Eggs (8 large)

2% milk (3 tbsp.)

Black pepper & salt (1/8 tsp. each)

Butter (3 tbsp.)

Mayo (.5 cup)

Split croissants (8)

Slices of tomato (8)

Ripe avocado (1 medium)

Directions:

Mince the jalapeno and mix with the cheese and herbs. Crumble in and mix with the sausage. Shape the mixture into eight patties.

Prepare the patties in a skillet using the medium temperature setting for four to five minutes per side. Keep them warm.

Whisk the milk, eggs, pepper, and salt. Prepare another skillet and melt half of the butter using the med-high temperature setting. Add half of the egg to the pan and swirl in the pan until fully cooked. Cover with a lid on the pot for one to two minutes.

Set the first eggs aside and repeat the process using the rest of the butter.

Slice the first batch into wedges.

Peel and slice the avocado.

Prepare the croissants with a portion of mayo, patty, eggs, avocado, and tomato. Replace the top and serve!

PANERA IN N' OUT BURGER

Preparation Time: 10 minutes

Cooking Time: 20 minutes

Servings: 8

Ingredients For the Patties:

1 ½ pound ground beef

1 ½ teaspoon salt

1 teaspoon ground black pepper

5 slices of American cheese

For the Sauce:

1/3 cup mayonnaise

1 tablespoon ketchup, sugar-free

1 teaspoon mustard paste

2 tablespoons diced pickles

2 teaspoons pickle juice

½ teaspoon salt

½ teaspoon paprika

½ teaspoon garlic powder

For the Toppings:

10 slices of tomato

20 lettuce leaves

10 pickles slices

½ of large white onion, peeled, sliced thin

Directions

Prepare the sauce and for this, take a small bowl, place all of its ingredients in it, whisk until mixed; set aside until required. Prepare the patties and for this, take a medium bowl, place beef in it, add salt and black pepper, stir until well combined, and then shape the mixture into ten balls. Take a griddle pan, place it over high heat, grease it with oil and when hot, place meatball on it, press them down and then cook 4 to 5 minutes per side until thoroughly cooked and browned. When done, place a cheese slice on top of one patty, stack with another patty, and repeat with the remaining patties. Assemble the burgers and for this, use two lettuce leaves as the bottom part of the bun, add some slices on onion, top with stacked burger patties, and then top with two slices of each tomato and pickles. Drizzle the prepared sauce over patties, and then cover the top with two lettuce leaves. Assemble the remaining burgers in the same manner and then serve.

IHOP SAUSAGE AND EGG BREAKFAST SANDWICH

Preparation Time: 10 minutes

Cooking Time: 30 minutes

Servings: 8

Ingredients: 4 sausage patties, cooked

6 slices of avocado

2 tablespoons mayonnaise

2 tablespoons butter, unsalted

4 slices of cheddar cheese

4 eggs

Directions

Take a large skillet pan, place it over medium heat, add butter, and then place flour egg molds or rings of mason jars in it. Crack an egg into each mold, break the yolks and whisk the egg by using a fork, then cover the pan with a lid and cook for 3 to 4 minutes until the egg has thoroughly cooked. Assemble the sandwich for this, place an egg onto a plate, spread 1 tablespoon of mayonnaise on top, top with one patty of sausage, a cheese slice, and three avocado slices, and then cover the top with another egg. Repeat to make another sandwich and then serve.

TGI Friday White Castle Copycat Hamburgers

Preparation Time: 10 minutes

Cooking Time: 20 minutes

Servings: 8

Ingredients:

1 1/2 lbs. of chuck, ground

1/3 cup of breadcrumbs, plain

1 egg, medium

1 x 1-oz. pkg. of soup mix, onion, dry

2 tbsp. of water, filtered

1/2 tsp. of pepper, ground

24 dinner rolls, square, small

Directions:

1. Preheat the oven to 400F.

2. Combine the ground chuck, egg, breadcrumbs, water, soup mix ground pepper in mixing bowl. Press into 15" x 10" pan. Prick holes in the chuck mixture to ventilate while it is cooking.

3. Bake chuck mixture in 400F oven till cooked through and browned, 10-12 minutes. Internal temperature should be 160F or higher. Drain off the excess grease.

4. Cut the mixture in squares about the same size as rolls. Place one patty in each dinner roll. Serve.

McDonald's McGriddle Breakfast Sandwich

Preparation Time: 10 minutes

Cooking Time: 20 minutes

Servings: 8

Ingredients:

½ cup maple syrup

1 cup flour

1 teaspoon baking powder

½ teaspoon baking soda

1 cup buttermilk

2 tablespoons butter, melted

1 egg

Softened butter for greasing the mold

4 slices American cheese

4 eggs, scrambled

4 strips bacon, cut in half and cook

Directions:

Line a baking tray with parchment paper and set aside.

Add maple syrup to a pot and bring to a boil over medium heat while stirring often. Keep stirring the syrup even when already boiling. At about 230 °F, after about a minute of boiling, the syrup will appear a bit darker, and the boiling will lessen to some degree. Cook until the syrup becomes darker and begins to smell a bit like caramel. It is ready to be removed from heat once it reaches 265 °F.

Pour maple syrup onto the prepared baking sheet. Spread evenly in a thin layer with a spatula. Refrigerate until cool. Flip the syrup over, with parchment paper now on top. Then, peel off the paper and break the solidified syrup into tiny pieces.

To make the pancakes, combine flour, baking powder, and baking soda in a large bowl. Set aside.

In another bowl, add buttermilk, butter, and egg. Mix until fully combined. Then, pour onto dry ingredients and mix well until incorporated.

Preheat electric grill to medium-high heat.

Coat insides of round molds with softened butter then place on a hot grill coated with butter over medium heat. Add about 2 tablespoons pancake batter into each mold then sprinkle maple crystals on top. Afterward, add 2 more tablespoons of pancake batter on top, sandwiching the maple crystals inside the pancakes.

Once bubbles form and edges look cooked, remove molds and flip pancakes. Additional 1 to 2 minutes to cook.

To assemble the sandwiches, add cheese, scrambles egg, bacon on the pancake, and top with another pancake.

Serve immediately.

McDonald's McGriddle Bacon Sandwiches

Preparation Time: 10 minutes

Cooking Time: 30 minutes

Servings: 8

Ingredients:

For the Buns:

1 cup almond flour

2 teaspoons leaven

½ teaspoon liquid stevia

1 ½ teaspoon erythritol sweetener

1 ½ teaspoon vanilla, unsweetened ½ cup pancake syrup, low-carb, sugar-free 3 ounces cheese, softened

3 eggs

For the Filling:

6 slices of bacon, cooked

½ teaspoon salt

½ teaspoon ground black pepper

6 slices of cheese

6 eggs

Directions:

Take a little saucepan, place it over medium-high heat, add pancake syrup, and convey it to a boil.

Continue boiling the syrup for 4 to eight minutes until reduced by half and thickened, stirring continuously, then spread the syrup on the baking pan lined with parchment paper and let it freeze for 1 hour.

Then turn on the oven, set it to 350 degrees F, and let it preheat.

Prepare the buns and for this, place all of its remaining ingredients into a blender then pulse for two minutes until smooth.

Take an outsized cooking utensil, line it with a foil, place 12 rings of jars, grease their insides with oil then evenly pour the blended batter for buns in them, 3 tablespoons per ring.

Remove the frozen syrup from the freezer, peel the parchment sheet, then cut syrup into small pieces and evenly distribute them into the batter within the rings.

Place the cooking utensil into the oven, bake for quarter-hour until the batter for buns has set, and when done, and allow them to cool within the cooking utensil for five minutes then remove buns from the rings to chill completely.

Meanwhile, prepare the filling for the buns, and for this, fry the eggs until cooked to the specified level and cook the bacon slices until crisp.

Assemble the sandwiches and for this, top each bun with a slice of bacon, a dish, a cheese slice, and then cover the highest with another bun.

Serve immediately.

Cheesecake Factory Cookie Dough & Ice Cream Sandwiches

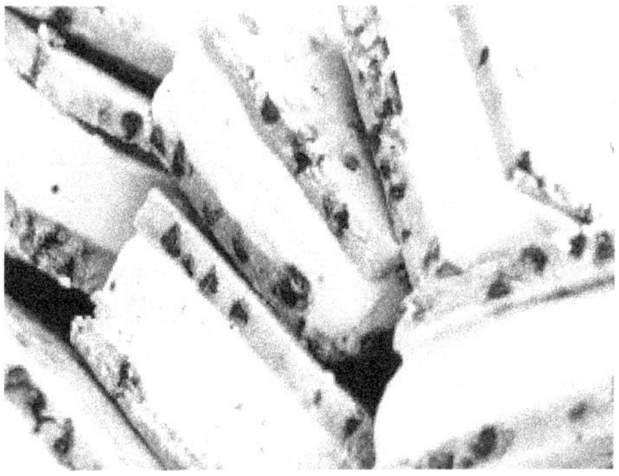

Preparation Time: 10 minutes

Cooking Time: 40 minutes

Servings: 8

Ingredients:

1 cup of butter

1 cup of packed brown sugar

¾ cup of sugar

¼ cup of milk

1 tsp of vanilla extract

2 ½ cups of all-purpose flour

1 tsp of salt

1 ½ cups of chocolate chips (some prefer shaved chocolate to this)

3 qt of soft vanilla ice cream

Directions:

Prepare a baking tray (or a tray that will fit into the freezer) by lining it with parchment paper (leave extra pieces hanging over the sides of the tray).

Melt the butter in a small bowl in the microwave. Let it cool down for a few minutes.

In a medium bowl, combine the melted butter, packed sugar, normal sugar, milk, and vanilla extract. Stir well to combine then add in the flour, salt, and chocolate chips.

Pour the dough into the tray, and press the dough down. Try to even it out as much as possible. Place the second layer of parchment paper over the top of the dough and place the tray in the freezer. Allow the dough to freeze for about 1 hour so that it sets nice and firmly.

Once the dough is ready, place the tray onto the counter. Find the center of the cookie dough (widthwise) and cut down the center of it.

Using an ice cream scooper (preferably), scoop, and layer ice cream onto the one half of the cookie dough.

Then carefully place the other half of the cookie dough layer (the one without ice cream) onto the other–to create the cookie and ice cream sandwich.

Pop the tray back into the freezer and freeze for at least 4 hours. Cut the cookie ice cream sandwich into small squares and serve.

Pro-tip: sprinkle some sprinkles or any of your favorite toppings on top of the sandwich to add more color.

CHAPTER 9:

Vegetarian and Salads Recipes

CAFÉ RIO'S BLACK BEANS

Preparation time: 10 minutes

Cooking time: 30 minutes

Servings: 8

Ingredients:

2 tablespoons olive oil

3 cloves garlic, minced

1 jalapeño pepper, minced

2 (15-ounce) cans black beans (one can drain, one with liquid)

2 teaspoons cumin

12 ounces' tomato juice

1 teaspoon salt

½ teaspoon black pepper

¼ cup chopped cilantro

Directions:

In a large nonstick skillet over medium heat, warm the oil and sauté the garlic and jalapeño until fragrant.

Add the beans and cumin. Simmer the mixture and cook for 5–10 minutes, until some of the liquid has evaporated.

Stir in the tomato juice, salt, pepper, and cilantro.

Cook to heat through, and serve.

El Charro's Chile Rellenos

Preparation time: 15 minutes

Cooking time: 40 minutes

Servings: 4

Ingredients:

For the chilies:

8 fresh green chills (with stems intact, if possible)

2 cups shredded cheddar

2 cups Monterey Jack cheese, shredded

For the batter:

3 eggs

3 tablespoons flour

1 teaspoon salt

1 teaspoon black pepper

For topping (optional):

4 cups taco sauce, warmed

1 cup shredded cheddar

1 cup shredded Monterey Jack cheese

Oil for frying

Directions:

Slice and core the peppers, leaving the stems on if possible. Stuff them with a mixture of the two kinds of cheese. Close the peppers around the cheese.

Heat the oil to 350°F.

Separate the eggs and beat the whites until stiff.

Beat the egg yolks and fold them into the whites, together with the flour, salt, and pepper.

Working with a few at a time, dip the peppers into the batter and carefully lower them into the hot oil. Cook on both sides until they are crisp and golden.

Heat the broiler to medium.

If desired, arrange the fried chills in a baking pan and pour the warm taco sauce over them. Add with the remaining broil and cheese until the cheese is melted and bubbly.

Rosa Mexicano's Mushroom Quesadillas

Preparation time: 10 minutes

Cooking time: 20 minutes

Servings: 6

Ingredients:

3 tablespoons olive oil

12 ounces mixed mushrooms (cremini, Portobello, shiitake, oyster), trimmed and thinly sliced

1 medium white onion, finely chopped

2 cloves, garlic, minced

2 serrano chilies, seeded, cored, and minced

¼ teaspoon salt

1 ½ cups shredded cheese (queso Chihuahua, Monterey Jack, or cheddar)

6 (6-inch) fresh corn tortillas

Optional sour cream and salsa Verde, for serving

Directions:

In a medium skillet, warm the oil over medium-high heat until it shimmers.

Add the mushrooms, onion, garlic, and chilies. Season with salt.

Cook for 8–10 minutes, or until the mushrooms are browned.

Transfer the filling mixture to a bowl and wipe out the skillet.

Reduce the heat to medium-low.

Divide the cheese among the tortillas leaving a small gap around the edges.

Spoon filling over half the tortilla and fold one side over the filling.

In batches, place the quesadillas in the hot skillet and cook on both sides until golden and crisp.

Serve with sour cream and salsa Verde, if desired.

Olive Garden Brussels Sprout N' Kale Salad

Preparation Time: 5 minutes

Cooking Time: 1 minute

Servings: 6

Ingredients:

1 bunch kale

1-pound Brussels sprouts

¼ cup raisins (or dry cranberries)

½ cup pecans, chopped

Maple vinaigrette:

½ cup olive oil

¼ cup apple cider vinegar

¼ cup maple syrup

1 teaspoon dry mustard

Directions:

Slice the kale and Brussels sprouts with a cheese grater or mandolin slicer. Transfer to a salad bowl.

Add the pecans to a skillet on high heat. Toast for 60 seconds, then transfer to the salad bowl. Add the raisins. Mix all of the ingredients for the vinaigrette and whisk to combine. Pour the vinaigrette over the salad and toss. Refrigerate for a few hours or preferably overnight before serving.

Abuelo's Jalapeño Cheese Fritters

Preparation time: 15 minutes

Cooking time: 15 minutes

Servings:40

Ingredients:

4 ounces' cream cheese, softened

6 cups shredded cheddar cheese

6 cups shredded Monterey Jack cheese

4 fresh jalapeños, deseeded and finely chopped

½ teaspoon Lawry's seasoning

Oil for frying

2 tablespoons all-purpose flour

2 eggs

½ cup water

3 cups breadcrumbs

Ranch dressing, for serving

Directions:

Combine the cream cheese, shredded cheeses, jalapeños, and seasoning in a mixing bowl, mix well.

Shape the mixture into balls using one level tablespoon for each. Place the balls on a baking sheet and set it in the fridge.

Heat the frying oil to 360°F. Set out a large baking sheet with a sheet of parchment and a platter with a paper towel.

Prepare your dipping station. In one bowl, place the flour. beat the eggs in the second bowl and mix in the water. Pour the breadcrumbs in a small baking pan or casserole dish.

Remove the cheese balls from the fridge. Working in small batches of 5–10 balls, drop them in the flour and toss to coat. Next, coat them with egg, and then breadcrumbs. Repeat the egg and breadcrumbs, and set them on the parchment-lined sheet.

Fry the cheese balls in batches for 1 to 1 ½ minutes, or until they are golden brown. Drain on a paper towel. Make sure to let the oil heat up again before adding more cheese balls.

Serve immediately with ranch dressing.

Caribbean Shrimp Salad

Preparation Time: 20 minutes

Cooking Time: 55 minutes

Servings: 4

Ingredients:

8 cups baby spinach, fresh

¼ cup lime juice, freshly squeezed

2 tablespoons chili garlic sauce

½ teaspoon paprika

4 cups cooked shrimp, chopped (approximately 1 ½ pounds)

1 tablespoon grated lime rind

5 tablespoons seasoned rice vinegar, divided

½ teaspoon ground cumin

1 cup peeled mango, chopped

½ cup green onions, thinly sliced

2 garlic cloves, minced

1 cup radishes, julienne-cut

¼ cup peeled avocado, diced

2 tablespoons pumpkinseed kernels, unsalted

1 ½ tablespoons olive oil

Dash of salt

Directions:

In a large bowl; combine the cooked shrimp with chili garlic sauce & 2 tablespoons of vinegar; toss well. Cover & let chill for an hour.

Now, in a small bowl; combine the leftover vinegar with garlic cloves, oil, lime juice, lime rind, ground cumin, paprika & salt; stirring well with a whisk.

Place 2 cups of spinach on each of 4 plates; top each serving with a cup of the prepared shrimp mixture. Arrange ¼ cup radishes, ¼ cup mango & 1 tablespoon of the avocado around the shrimp on each plate. Top each serving with approximately 1 ½ teaspoons of pumpkinseed kernels & 2 tablespoons of green onions. Drizzle each salad with approximately 2 tablespoons of the vinaigrette. Serve and enjoy.

Chipotle's Sofritas

Preparation time: 10 minutes

Cooking time 25 minutes

Servings: 2

Ingredients:

Mexican Spice Mix:

½ teaspoon dried oregano leaves

2 teaspoons ancho chili powder, ground

1 teaspoon cumin, ground

½ teaspoon coriander, ground

½ teaspoon kosher salt

Sofritas:

1 tablespoon avocado or olive oil

½ medium onion, diced

2 garlic cloves, minced

1 teaspoon chipotle chili in adobo sauce, minced

1 tablespoon mild Hatch chili, diced

1 tablespoon Mexican Spice Mix

2 tablespoons tomato paste

1 package (16-ounces) organic extra firm tofu, drained, dried, crumbled

1 cup of your favorite Mexican beer

Salt and black pepper to taste

Tortillas and lime wedges for garnish

Directions:

Place all the Mexican Spice Mix ingredients in a container or plastic bag and shake to mix.

Sauté the onion and garlic in oil over medium heat for 5 minutes.

Mix in both the chilies and the spice mix and sauté for another minute.

Pour in the tomato paste and cook for a minute.

Add the rest of the ingredients and cook for 5 more minutes. Adjust and taste seasoning with pepper and salt if required.

Remove the mixture from heat, transfer to a bowl, and then serve with tortillas and thin lime wedges.

Cracker Barrel Quesadilla Explosion Salad

Preparation Time: 20 minutes

Cooking Time: 20 minutes

Servings: 1

Ingredients:

1 vegetarian chicken patty

6 ounces bagged salad mix

For Chipotle Ranch Dressing:

1 cup 2% milk

1 packet ranch dressing mix

1 teaspoon chipotle peppers in adobo sauce

1 cup non-fat Greek yogurt

For Citrus Balsamic Vinaigrette

2 tablespoon balsamic vinegar

½ teaspoon orange zest

2 tablespoon Splenda

¼ cup orange juice

A pinch of nutmeg

For Sweet Potato Strips:

¼ medium sweet potato, washed, thinly sliced & cut into strips

nonstick cooking spray

¼ teaspoon salt

For Roasted Corn and Black Bean Salsa:

1 cup black beans, rinsed

2 ears of corn, roasted, kernels removed from the cob

½ cup fresh cilantro, chopped

1 tablespoon lime juice, freshly squeezed

¼ red onion, chopped

1 jalapeno pepper, roasted, peeled, seeded, deveined & chopped

Salt to taste

1 red bell pepper, medium, roasted, peeled, seeded & chopped

Directions:

For Sweet Potato Strips:

Preheat oven to 350 F. Lightly coat the strips with nonstick cooking spray and then, dust them lightly with the salt. Place on a large-sized cookie sheet in a single layer & bake for 15 to 20 minutes. Don't forget to stir the strips & turn halfway during the baking process.

Set aside and let cool until ready to use.

For Roasted Corn Salsa:

Add corn together with peppers & black beans to a large bowl and then squeeze the lime juice on top; add salt to taste. Give the ingredients a good stir & add the fresh cilantro.

For Chipotle Ranch Dressing:

Add yogurt and milk to the ranch dressing mix. Stir in the chipotle & store in a refrigerator.

For Citrus Balsamic Vinaigrette:

Over low heat in a large saucepan; place the entire ingredients together & cook for a minute. Set aside and let cool then refrigerate.

For Quesadilla:

1. Place the cheese on half of the tortilla & then fold over.

Lightly coat the tortilla with the nonstick cooking spray & then cook over medium-high heat in a large pan. Cook until the cheese is completely melted, for a minute per side. Cut into 4 wedges.

Prepare the veggie "chicken" patty as per the directions mentioned on the package & then slice into thin strips.

Place approximately 6 ounces of the salad mix on the plate and then top with the "chicken" strips, black bean salsa, sweet potato strips & roasted corn.

Place the cut quesadilla around the edge of the plate and then drizzle the salad with the prepared dressings.

SPINACH ARTICHOKE DIP

Preparation Time: 15 minutes

Cooking Time: 10 minutes

Servings: 8

Ingredients:

Salt and pepper to taste

3 tablespoons butter

3 tablespoons flour

1½ cups milk

½ teaspoon salt

¼ teaspoon black pepper

5 ounces' spinach, chopped and frozen

¼ cup artichokes, diced marinated

½ cup parmesan, shredded

½ cup mozzarella, shredded

1 tablespoon Romano cheese, shredded

¼ cup mozzarella cheese (for topping)

1 tablespoon asiago cheese, shredded

½ teaspoon garlic, chopped

2 tablespoons cream cheese

Directions:

Preheat oven to 425 ° F.

When the puff pastry is completely thawed, unfold each sheet to a size of 12 inches by 12 inches. Cut the leaves into quarters.

Combine sugar, crumbs, cinnamon, and nutmeg in a small bowl. Brush one of the puff pastry squares with some of the beaten eggs. Add about 1 tablespoon of bread mixture on top, then add half an apple, core down, over the crumbs. Add another tablespoon of bread mix Seal the dough by pulling on the corners and pressing the dough until the seams are completely sealed. Repeat this process with the other squares. Collect ingredients for stressful nuts in a small bowl Grease a baking sheet or line it with parchment. Place the bouquets on the sheet and brush with a little more beaten egg. Top with sterile walnuts. Bake for 15 minutes and then reduce the temperature to 350. F and bake for an additional 25 minutes or until lightly browned. Prepare the ice cream by combining the sugar, vanilla, and confectionery milk until it reaches the proper consistency. When the cookies are ready, let them cool to room temperature and sprinkle ice before serving.

Chili Santa Fe Crispers Salad

Preparation Time: 10 minutes

Cooking Time: 30 minutes

Servings: 4

Ingredients:

1 ½ pounds boneless skinless chicken breasts

1 tablespoon fresh cilantro, chopped

¾ cup Lawry's Santa Fe Chili Marinated with Lime and Garlic, divided

1 package (10 ounces) torn romaine lettuce, approximately 8 cups

2 tablespoons milk 1 cup black beans, drained and rinsed

½ cup sour cream 1 cup drained canned whole kernel corn

¼ cup red onion, chopped

1 medium avocado, cut into chunks

½ cup Monterey Jack, shredded

1 medium tomato, cut into chunks

Directions:

Place chicken in a large glass dish or resealable marinade plastic bag

Add approximately ½ cup of the Santa Fe marinade, turn several times until nicely coated

Refrigerate for 30 minutes or longer

Removed the chicken from marinade; get rid of the leftover marinade

Grill the chicken until cooked through, for 6 to 7 minutes per side, over medium heat; brush with 2 tablespoons of the leftover marinade

Cut the chicken into thin slices.

Combine the sour cream with milk, leftover marinade, and cilantro with wire whisk in a medium-sized bowl until smooth

Arrange lettuce on a large serving platter

Top with the chicken, avocado, corn, beans, cheese, tomato, and onion.

Serve with tortilla chips and dressing. Enjoy.

CHAPTER 10:

Dessert Recipes

IHOP COUNTRY GRIDDLE CAKES

Preparation time: 5 minutes

Cooking time: 10 minutes

Serving: 8-10

Ingredients:

2 teaspoons of salt

¼ cup of vegetable oil

1 teaspoon of baking soda

1 teaspoon of baking powder

⅓ cup of granulated sugar

1 egg

⅓ cup of instant Cream of Wheat (dry)

1 ½ cups of buttermilk

1 ¼ cups of all-purpose flour

Nonstick spray

Direction:

Take a frying pan, coat the surface of it with nonstick spray, and place it over medium heat.

Use a large bowl to mix all the ingredients using an electric mixer on medium speed. Blend until you get a smooth mixture.

Take portions of ⅓ cup of batter and put them in the pan—Cook the pancakes between 1 to 3 minutes (or until the base turns golden brown). Flip to cook on the other side for about the same amount of time, or until it turns golden brown. Repeat the process for the remaining batter. Serve warm.

CHEESECAKE FACTORY APPLE CHIMI CHEESECAKE

Preparation Time: 10 minutes

Cooking time: 10 minutes

Servings: 2

Ingredients:

2 (9 inches) flour tortillas

¼ cup granulated sugar

½ teaspoon cinnamon

3 ounces' cream cheese, softened

½ teaspoon vanilla extract

⅓ cup apple, peeled and finely chopped

Oil for frying

Vanilla ice cream (optional)

Caramel topping (optional)

Directions:

Make sure your tortillas and cream cheese are at room temperature; this will make them both easier to work with.

In a small bowl, combine the sugar and cinnamon.

In another mixing bowl, combine the cream cheese and vanilla until smooth. Fold in the apple.

Divide the apple and cheese mixture in two and place half in the center of each tortilla. Leave at least an inch margin around the outside.

Fold the tortilla top to the middle, then the bottom to the middle, and then roll it up from the sides.

Heat about half an inch of oil in a skillet over medium heat.

Place the filled tortillas into the skillet and fry on each side until they are golden brown. Transfer them to a paper towel-lined plate to drain any excess oil, then immediately coat them with the cinnamon and sugar.

Serve with a scoop of ice cream.

APPLEBEE'S CHOCOLATE MOUSSE DESSERT SHOOTER

Preparation time: 10 minutes

Cooking time: 20 minutes

Serving: 4

Ingredients:

Canned whipped cream

½ cup of chocolate fudge sauce

8 Oreo cookies

½ cup of heavy cream

2 tablespoons of brown sugar

2 eggs, separated

1 teaspoon of vanilla extract

1 tablespoon of Godiva Chocolate Liqueur

6 ounces of semisweet chocolate chips (or 1 cup)

2 tablespoons of salted butter

Directions:

Prepare a double boiler by placing a metal bowl inside a medium skillet over low heat. Fill the skillet with a couple of inches of water, and let it heat while you put a piece of butter in the metal bowl. After the butter has melted, you can add the chocolate chips, leaving at least 1 tablespoon of them aside. After the chocolate melts, add the vanilla and chocolate liqueur. Take the metal bowl out of the skillet and whisk in the egg yolks. Use a separate bowl to whisk the egg whites until you get soft peaks. Pour this mixture into the other mixture and stir. Use another medium bowl to mix sugar and cream. Whip the cream until it gets stiff. Add the whipped cream into the chocolate mixture. The remaining chocolate chips have to be chopped into small bits (the size of rice), stir them into the mousse, and cover it for 3 to 4 hours to cool down. Empty the filling of the Oreos, place the chocolate cookies into a plastic bag, and pound on it until you get a bag full of crumbs (you can use a kitchen mallet for this task). Use 6-ounce rock glasses for each serving. Spoon 2 tablespoons of Oreo crumbs into the bottom of each glass, add ⅓ cup of chilled mousse, and top it off with two tablespoons of chocolate fudge. It's easier to heat the fudge into the microwave first before spooning it into a glass. Add some whipped cream on top and some leftover Oreo crumbs.

Applebee's Key Lime Pie Dessert Shooter

Preparation time: 10 minutes

Cooking time: 20 minutes

Serving: 4

Key Lime Filling Ingredients:

½ cup of key lime juice

14 ounces of condensed milk

4 egg yolks

Key Lime Topping Ingredients:

Canned whipped cream

½ cup plus 2 teaspoons of graham cracker crumbs

3 tablespoons of powdered sugar

2 teaspoons of key lime juice

½ cup of sour cream

Directions:

Use a medium bowl and an electric mixer to beat the egg yolks on high speed for about 2 to 3 minutes or light yellow. Add the condensed milk and mix for 30 more seconds. Pour the mixture into a medium pan that was placed over medium-low heat, and stir in ½ cup of key lime juice. Cook for 8 to 10 minutes and stir very often, until you notice the mixture starting to bubble. Remove over the heat and let it cool for about 3 to 4 hours.

Prepare the key lime topping by mixing key lime juice, powdered sugar, and sour cream. Cover the topping and let it cool.

For each serving, prepare a 6-ounce rock glass, spoon 2 tablespoons of graham cracker crumbs into it, add ½ cup of key lime filling, and add 2 tablespoons of topping on top.

Add whipped cream on top, sprinkle about ½ teaspoon of crumbs on it, and enjoy.

McDonald Cinnamon Apple Turnover

Preparation Time: 10 minutes Cooking time:25 minutes

Servings: 6

Ingredients:

1 large Granny Smith apple, peeled, cored, and diced

½ teaspoon cornstarch

¼ teaspoon cinnamon

Dash ground nutmeg

¼ cup brown sugar

¼ cup applesauce

¼ teaspoon vanilla extract

1 tablespoon butter, melted

1 sheet of puff pastry, thawed

Whipped cream or vanilla ice cream, to serve

Directions:

Preheat the oven to 400°F.

Prepare a baking sheet by spraying it with nonstick cooking spray or using a bit of oil on a paper towel.

In a mixing bowl, mix the apples, cornstarch, cinnamon, nutmeg, and brown sugar. Stir to make sure the apples are well covered with the spices. Then stir in the applesauce and the vanilla.

Layout your puff pastry and cut it into squares. You should be able to make 4 or 6 depending on how big you want your turnovers to be and how big your pastry is.

Place some of the apple mixtures in the center of each square and fold the corners of the pastry up to make a pocket. Pinch the edges together to seal. Then brush a bit of the melted butter over the top to give the turnovers that nice brown color.

Place the filled pastry onto the prepared baking pan and transfer it to the preheated oven. Bake 20–25 minutes, or until they become a golden brown.

Serve with whipped cream or vanilla ice cream.

PANERA BANANA PUDDING

Preparation Time: 15 minutes

Cooking time 5 minutes

Servings: 10

Ingredients:

6 cups milk

5 eggs, beaten

¼ teaspoon vanilla extract

1⅛ cups flour

1½ cups sugar

¾ pound vanilla wafers

3 bananas, peeled

8 ounces Cool Whip or 2 cups of whipped cream

Directions:

In a large saucepan, heat the milk to about 170°F.

Mix the eggs, vanilla, flour, and sugar in a large bowl.

Layer banana slices over the top of the vanilla wafers. Be as liberal with the bananas as you want.

Layer the custard mixture on top of the wafers and bananas. Move the pan to the refrigerator and cool for 1½ hours. When ready to serve, spread Cool Whip (or real whipped cream, if you prefer) over the top. Garnish with banana slices and wafers if desired.

TGI FRIDAY MOLTEN CHOCOLATE CAKE

Preparation Time: 1 hour 30 minutes

Cooking Time: 30 minutes

Servings: 10

Ingredients:

1 Duncan Hines fudge cake mix

3 large eggs

1 cup milk

½ cup oil

½ cup sour cream

Vanilla ice cream

Chocolate shell ice cream topping

Caramel sauce

For Magic Shell

¼ cup coconut oil

2 cups chocolate chips, semisweet

For Hot Fudge

1 bag semisweet chocolate chips (12-ounces)

4 tablespoons unsalted butter

1 can sweeten condensed milk (14-ounces)

A pinch of salt

1 teaspoon pure vanilla extract

Directions:

Stir the dry cake mix together with sour cream, eggs, milk & oil in a large bowl.

Lightly coat a large-sized cupcake pan with the nonstick spray & distribute the batter evenly approximately ¾ full. Bake as per the directions mentioned on the package.

Turn the cakes out onto their tops creating a "volcano" & let cool.

Gently cut a hole out of the middle without going clear to the bottom using a pairing or serrated knife.

Fill with cool hot fudge & then slice off the bottom circle of the piece of cake you removed and place it on the hot fudge hole like a lid.

Using a plastic wrap; cover & let chill in a fridge for 30 minutes.

Remove the cakes from the freezer & reheat in the microwave for half a minute, until warm.

Top with caramel, ice cream & magic shell.

For Magic Shell:

Place the chocolate along with the coconut oil in a microwave-safe bowl and slowly heat for 30-second intervals until melted, stirring often.

Serve over ice cream & it would harden.

For Hot Fudge:

Melt the entire ingredients together over medium heat in a medium saucepan.

Bring the mixture to a boil, stirring now and then.

Continue to boil & stir for a minute or two more.

Remove the pan from heat & continue to stir for a minute.

Let the fudge sauce to cool.

CHAPTER 11:

Drink Recipes

WENDY'S COPYCAT CHOCOLATE FROSTY

Preparation Time: 10 minutes

Cooking Time: 20 minutes

Servings: 8

Ingredients:

½ cup chocolate syrup

2 cups whole milk

1 (7-ounce) can sweeten condensed milk

½ teaspoon vanilla extract

½ cup heavy cream

Directions

Combine the chocolate syrup, whole milk, and condensed milk in a mixing bowl. Refrigerate for 1 hour until chilled.

To another mixing bowl, add the heavy cream and vanilla. Beat well until soft peaks form. Chill in the refrigerator.

Prepare your ice cream maker and add the chocolate mixture to the ice cream making bowl.

Prepare ice cream as per directions (it will take about 15–20 minutes to churn it).

Turn off the machine, take out the paddles, and add the cream mixture to the bowl. Combine well.

Serve chilled, or place in the freezer until frozen to the desired consistency.

JAMBA JUICE'S COPYCAT RAZZMATAZZ SMOOTHIE

Preparation Time: 10 minutes

Cooking Time: 30 minutes

Servings: 8

Ingredients:

1 cup frozen strawberries

½ banana, sliced

1 cup orange sherbet

1 cup raspberry juice

1 cup ice

Directions

Add the ice and other ingredients to a blender or food processor.

Blend until the mixture is smooth.

Serve chilled.

TGI FRIDAY'S COPYCAT TROPICAL RUNNER SMOOTHIE

Preparation Time: 10 minutes

Cooking Time: 20 minutes

Servings: 8

Ingredients:

1 (8-ounce)) can crushed pineapple, with juice

1 banana

½ cup orange sherbet

½ cup liquid Piña Colada mix

2 cups ice

Directions

Slice the banana in half and then cut to make ¼-inch slices. Set aside two slices.

Add the remaining slices, pineapple with juice, Piña Colada mix, orange sherbet, and ice to a blender or food processor.

Blend for 15–30 seconds until the mixture is smooth and creamy.

Pour into two glasses.

Garnish with banana slices and serve chilled.

JAMBA PASSION ICED TEA LEMONADE

Preparation Time: 10 minutes

Cooking Time: 10 minutes

Servings: 8

Ingredients:

2 tablespoons granulated sugar

1 cup prepared lemonade

1 Tazo Passion teabag

Water

Ice

Directions

Over moderate heat settings in a large pot, heat one cup of water until starts boiling.

Now, combine 2 tablespoons sugar with 1 tablespoon of water in a small-sized microwave-safe bowl & prepare the sugar syrup. Microwave the bowl on high for half a minute, uncovered. Stir well until the sugar dissolves completely; set aside.

Place the teabag in a large-sized heat-proof glass & measure a cup of hot boiling water & then steep tea. Once the tea has steeped for 4 to 5 minutes, remove & discard the tea bag; set aside & let cool for 10 to 15 minutes at room temperature. Transfer lemonade and tea in a medium-sized serving glass & top it with ice cubes. Add some teaspoons of sugar syrup; combine well with lemonade & iced brewed tea. Serve immediately.

JAMBA MANGO DRAGON FRUIT REFRESHER

Preparation Time: 10 minutes

Cooking Time: 20 minutes

Servings: 8

Ingredients:

1/2 cup of fresh red dragon fruit, cut into small pieces

2 cups of ice

4 ounces of mango juice

8 ounces white grape juice

Directions

Combine all the ingredients in a shaker. Shake everything together to break the dragon fruit, about 30 seconds.

Iced Chai Latte for 4

Ingredients

8 Chai teabags

Milk (to taste)

8 cups water

Directions

Over moderate heat settings in a large pot, boil the water & then add in the tea bags. Let seep for half an hour.

Remove the tea bags & before you add it to a pitcher; let it cool. Let chill in a refrigerator or fridge overnight.

Transfer half glass of the chai mix & top it with the milk. Add in the ice cubes; stir several times. Serve & enjoy.

Jamba Frozen Caramel Macchiato

Preparation Time: 15 minutes

Cooking Time: 5 minutes

Servings: 1

Ingredients:

4 tablespoons whipped topping

1 cup whole milk, ice-cold

2 fluid ounces original Starbucks whole bean espresso coffee or brewed Starbucks espresso

2 -3 tablespoons buttery rich caramel syrup, thick

2 tablespoons vanilla syrup

8 ice cubes

2 tablespoons half & half

Directions

First, brew the Starbucks espresso shot. Now, fill a large glass with ice; leaving approximately 2 inches from the top; add in the whole milk and then pour 2 tablespoons of heavy cream or half & half. Now add vanilla syrup & brewed Starbucks whole bean espresso on top of the milk. Drizzle the indoor of your glass with thick caramel syrup & top with whipped cream; lastly, drizzle a small amount of caramel syrup more over the top.

Jamba S'mores Frappuccino

Preparation Time: 10 minutes

Cooking Time: 20 minutes

Servings: 8

Ingredients:

2 tablespoons marshmallow fluff

1-2 tablespoons chocolate syrup

1 cup vanilla ice cream

1/2 cup milk

¼ cup cold coffee

2 tablespoons flavored s'mores syrup

1 cup ice

1 tablespoon whipped cream

1 graham cracker

Directions

In a large glass place two scoops of marshmallow fluff and top with some chocolate syrup. In a blender mix ice, milk, ice cream, coffee, and syrup until smooth. Pour in the glass. Top with whipped cream and drizzle chocolate syrup and crushed graham crackers. Note: replace ice with a frozen banana for an interesting change-up.

JAMBA CHESTNUT PRALINE FRAPPUCCINO FOR 4

Preparation Time: 10 minutes

Cooking Time: 20 minutes

Servings: 4

Ingredients:

Chestnut syrup:

2 baked chestnuts

½ cup brown sugar

¾ cup water

½ tablespoon vanilla paste

Praline crumble:

¼ cup pecan halves

2 tablespoons coconut sugar

2 tablespoons brown sugar

3 tablespoons water

Additional:

½ cup strong coffee

½ cup steamed milk

Whipped cream, as desired

Directions

Make the syrup; Chop the chestnuts and place in a food processor.

Process until finely chopped.

Combine water and brown sugar in a saucepot.

Simmer the mixture over medium-high heat until the sugar is dissolved.

Let the syrup cool a bit and pour it into a food processor.

Add vanilla paste and process until you have a smooth syrup.

Make the praline crumble; preheat oven to 350F.

Combine coconut sugar, brown sugar, and water in a saucepot.

Bring to a simmer over medium-high heat.

Once the sugar is dissolved, add pecans. Spread the mixture over a baking sheet lined with parchment paper.

Bake in the heated oven for 10 minutes. Place on a wire rack to cool down.

Transfer into a food processor and process until coarse. Assemble; Add 1 tablespoon syrup in a glass. Add some coffee and steamed milk.

Top with whipped cream and decorate with pecan praline.

Serve.

CHAPTER 12:

Timeless Restaurant Favorite Recipes

CHEESECAKE FACTORY CHEESY GARLIC BREADSTICKS

Preparation Time: 15 minutes

Cooking Time: 17 minutes

Servings: *4*

Ingredients*:*

1 pizza dough, pre-made crust

½ loaf white bread, thawed

1 tablespoon butter, salted

⅔ teaspoon minced well-cooked

¼ teaspoon salt

¼ teaspoon garlic powder

¼ teaspoon dried parsley

⅛ teaspoon dried basil

⅛ teaspoon dried oregano

¼ tablespoon grated parmesan

1 cup shredded mozzarella cheese

Directions:

Take a pizza pan and grease it with cooking oil;

Remove the pizza dough from the packet and spread it into the pizza pan;

Cover this pizza pan with plastic wrap and leave the crust for 5 hours at room temperature to thaw;

Set the oven temperature at 425 degrees F to preheat;

Now take a small bowl and add butter;

Place this butter bowl in the microwave and heat for 1 minute until the butter is melted;

Add minced garlic to the melted butter;

Mix these ingredients well;

Gently brush this butter garlic mixture over the pizza crust;

Take another small bowl and add parsley, garlic powder, salt, oregano, parmesan, and basil;

Mix these ingredients then sprinkle over the butter layer;

Finally, spread shredded mozzarella cheese over the crust;

Leave the crust for 30 minutes at room temperature;

Now bake the crust in the preheated oven at 425 degrees F for 15 minutes approximately;

Slice the crust into breadsticks;

Garnish with dried herbs if desired;

Serve fresh with your favorite sauce and dip.

Texas Roadhouse Parmesan Bread Bites

Preparation Time: 15 minutes

Cooking Time: 14 minutes

Servings: **4**

Ingredients:

½ (13.8 oz. tube) refrigerated classic pizza crust

3 tablespoons melted butter

½ teaspoon garlic salt

3 tablespoons parmesan cheese, grated

¼ teaspoon dried parsley

⅓ cup marinara sauce

Directions:

Switch on the oven and set its temperature at 350 degrees F;

Remove the pizza dough from the packet and unroll it into on the working surface;

Slice the pizza dough into 3 equal-sized pieces;

Shape each piece into 1 ½-inch thick log and cut each log into 1-inch long pieces;

Take a baking sheet and spread a wax paper in this baking sheet;

Place the dough pieces in the baking sheet;

Brush all the dough pieces with melted butter;

Sprinkle half of the garlic salt and parmesan cheese on top;

Bake them for 14 minutes in the preheated oven;

Mix the remaining garlic salt with parsley and remaining butter in a small bowl;

Remove the baked bread bites from the oven;

Sprinkle parmesan cheese over the freshly baked bread bites;

Leave the cheese bites at room temperature for 5 minutes;

Serve the bites with marinara sauce or cheesy dips;

Enjoy.

Deep-Fried Pickles from Texas Roadhouse

Preparation Time: 10 minutes

Cooking Time: 10 minutes

Servings: 4

Ingredients:

Vegetable oil, for deep frying

¼ cup flour

1¼ teaspoons Cajun seasoning, divided

¼ teaspoon oregano

¼ teaspoon basil

⅛ teaspoon cayenne pepper

Kosher salt

2 cups dill pickles, drained and sliced

¼ cup mayonnaise

1 tablespoon horseradish

1 tablespoon ketchup

Directions:

Preheat about 1½ inches oil to 375°F in a large pot.

In a separate bowl, make the coating by combining flour, 1 teaspoon Cajun seasoning, oregano, basil, cayenne pepper, and Kosher salt.

Dredge pickle slices in flour mixture. Lightly shake to remove any excess, then carefully lower into the hot oil. Work in batches to not overcrowd the pot. Deep fry for about 2 minutes or until lightly brown.

Using a slotted spoon, transfer pickles to a plate lined with paper towels to drain.

While pickles drain and cool, add mayonnaise, horseradish, ketchup, and remaining Cajun seasoning in a bowl. Mix well.

Serve immediately with dip on the side.

The Famous Breadsticks from Olive Garden

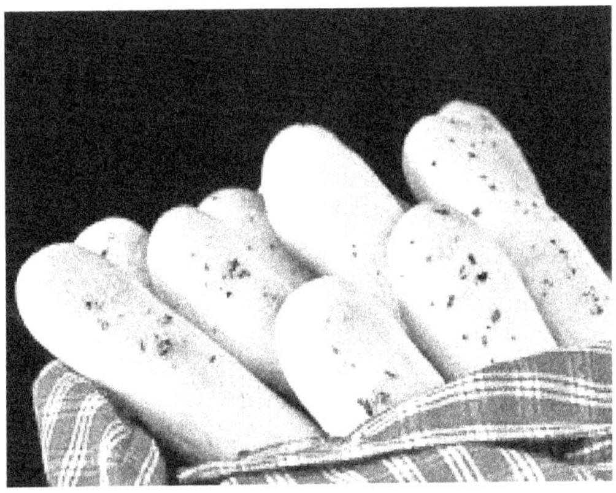

Preparation Time: 15 minutes

Cooking Time: 15 minutes

Servings: 16

Ingredients:

1½ cups plus 2 tablespoons warm water

1 package active dry yeast

4¼ cups all-purpose flour, plus more for dusting

2 tablespoons unsalted butter, softened

2 tablespoons sugar

1 tablespoon fine salt

3 tablespoons unsalted butter, melted

½ teaspoon kosher salt

¼ teaspoon garlic powder

Pinch dried oregano

Directions:

Preheat oven to 400°F. Prepare a baking tray and line it with parchment paper.

To prepare the dough, pour ¼ cup warm water in a mixing bowl. Add yeast and wait 5 minutes or until bubbles form. Combine with flour, 2 tablespoons butter, sugar, salt, and 1¼ cups and 2 tablespoons warm water. Mix for about 5 minutes or until the mixture turns into a dough that is a bit sticky.

Remove from bowl and transfer onto a flat surface sprinkled with flour. Knead for about 3 minutes until the dough is soft and smooth. Form dough into a log that is about 2 feet long. Then, cut dough equally in 1½-inch long pieces, making 16 small pieces in total. For each piece, knead slightly and form into a breadstick that is about 7 inches long. Position breadsticks on a prepared baking tray with 2-inch spaces in between each. Cover, then set aside for 45 minutes or until dough size has doubled.

Using a brush, coat breadsticks with 1½ tablespoons melted butter. Season with ¼ teaspoon salt.

Place in oven and bake for 15 minutes or until slightly golden.

As the breadsticks bake, mix remaining salt, garlic powder, and oregano in a bowl.

Remove breadsticks from the oven and immediately coat with the rest of the melted butter. Season with herb mixture.

Serve warm.

TACO BELL PASTA CARBONARA

Preparation Time: 20 minutes

Cooking Time: 40 minutes

Servings: 4

Ingredients:

½ lb. linguine pasta

3 bacon strips, chopped

½ cup frozen peas

1 tablespoon lemon juice, freshly squeezed

⅔ teaspoon grated lemon zest

1 large egg, beaten

1 tablespoon fresh parsley, chopped

¼ cup Parmigiano-Reggiano cheese, grated

¼ teaspoon salt, or to taste

⅛ teaspoon pepper, or to taste

Grated Parmigiano-Reggiano cheese, to serve

Directions:

Remove the linguine pasta from its box and keep it in a tray;

Take a large-sized saucepan and fill it with water;

Place the saucepan over medium heat and add pasta to cook according to the package directions ;

Check when the pasta is well-cooked then remove the saucepan from the heat;

Drain the pasta and keep it warm. Preserve the pasta water;

Now take a large and deep skillet and place it over medium heat;

Add bacon to this skillet and cook it until brown and crispy;

Drain excess bacon fats from the skillet;

Toss in peas and cook for about 5 minutes until they are warm through;

Meanwhile, blend Reggiano cheese, salt, black pepper, egg, lemon juice, and lemon zest in a blender until smooth and creamy;

Pour this sauce into the peas and stir well;

Add boiled pasta to the bacon pan and mix well;

Transfer the pasta to the serving bowl or plate;

Garnish the bacon pasta with cheese shreds;

Serve warm.

CHILI MEATBALL SUB

Preparation Time: 10 minutes

Cooking Time: 20 minutes

Servings: 4

Ingredients:

1 ½ large eggs, lightly beaten

2 tablespoons whole milk

⅔ medium onion, chopped

1 ½ garlic cloves, minced

⅔ cup soft breadcrumbs

⅓ teaspoon salt

teaspoon Italian seasoning

⅔ lb. bulk Italian sausage, the meat removed from the skin

¼ lb. ground beef

1 ½ jar (26 oz.) spaghetti sauce

½ loaf (1 lb.) unsliced French bread, halved lengthwise

4 slices part-skim mozzarella cheese

Shredded Parmesan cheese, to serve

Directions:

Mix the Italian sausage meat and beef in a bowl. Chop onions and garlic, then keep them aside;

Beat eggs with onion, milk, garlic, salt, Italians seasoning, and breadcrumbs in a bowl; Add beef and sausage to the egg mixture and mix well; Make 1-inch balls out of this beef mixture and place those balls in a baking tray; Slightly flatten the balls and bake them for 15 minutes at 425 degrees F until golden brown; Place a medium-sized Dutch oven over medium heat and add spaghetti sauce; Heat the sauce to a simmer, then add meatballs and cook for approximately 15 minutes; Cut the bread into 2 halves and keep the bottom half on the working surface; Spread the meatballs mixture over the bottom half of the bread; Top the meatballs with mozzarella cheese; Place the remaining bread slice on top; Press the 2 slices together and place the sandwiches in the serving plates; Top with shredded Parmesan cheese and serve warm and fresh with your favorite salad.

P.F. Chang Beef Tenderloin in Mushroom Sauce

Preparation Time: 15 minutes

Cooking Time: 25 minutes

Servings: 4

Ingredients:

8 tablespoons butter

2 teaspoons canola oil

4 beef tenderloin steaks, 1-inch thick

2 cups sliced fresh mushrooms

2 tablespoons chopped green onion

2 tablespoons all-purpose flour

¼ teaspoon salt

Dash of black pepper

1 ½ cups chicken broth

¼ teaspoon browning sauce

Directions:

Place the tenderloin steaks on the working surface;

Make sure that each steak is 1-inch thick and trim off excess fat;

Pat the steaks dry with a paper towel;

Take a large skillet and place it over medium-high heat;

Add 2 tablespoons butter along with oil and heat it for 30 seconds;

Place the steaks in the skillet and cook for 6 minutes per side until it is cooked medium-rare;

Remove the steak from the skillet and leave its drippings in the pan;

Add remaining butter to the same pan and heat it over medium-high heat;

Stir in mushrooms, and green onion, and sauté until soft and tender;

Add black pepper, salt, and flour and cook for 30 seconds, stirring continuously;

Slowly pour in the broth and whisk well until flour is mixed and incorporated;

Cook the sauce for 2 minutes while whisking continuously until it turns golden brown;

Place the cooked steaks in the serving plates;

Pour the mushroom sauce over the steaks;

Serve warm with your favorite salad or side dish.

Texas Roadhouse Herb Chicken Mediterranean Pizza

Preparation Time: 25 minutes

Cooking Time: 34 minutes

Servings: 4

Ingredients:

1 Pillsbury thin crust pizza dough

1 chicken breast, sliced

Salt and black pepper, to taste

6 tablespoons pure olive oil separated

2 tablespoons minced garlic

1 ½ cups mozzarella cheese grated

½ cup feta cheese crumbles

½ cup sundried tomatoes

1 cup spinach leaves

Directions:

Switch on the oven and set its temperature at 400 degrees F to preheat;

Take a sauté pan and place it over the medium heat;

Add 3 tablespoons of oil to the saucepan and let it heat up;

Toss the chicken slices with salt, and black pepper then place in the saucepan;

Cook the pepper chicken for 5 minutes per side or more until the chicken is well-cooked;

Remove this chicken and transfer to a plate;

Spray a cookie sheet with cooking oil and place the pizza dough on this cookie sheet;

Flatten the dough and brush it with 3 tablespoons olive oil;

Rub the pizza dough with minced garlic;

Evenly spread the garlic over the dough;

Leave it for 10 minutes at room temperature;

Sprinkle mozzarella cheese over the prepared pizza dough;

Spread spinach leaves, sundried tomatoes, feta cheese crumbles, and cooked chicken over the pizza dough;

Place the pizza in the preheated oven;

Bake the spinach pizza for 14 minutes until golden brown;

Cut the pizza into slices;

Serve warm.

Conclusion

Thank you for making it through to the end of *Copycat Cookbook*, let's hope it was informative and able to provide you with all of the tools you need to achieve your goals whatever they may be.

Hopefully, these recipes help to comfort all your possible fast food cravings, and that you find a few new recipes that you'll use quite often in the future! It's also important to remember all of these recipes can be altered/experimented with, to match your taste. Try these recipes and make them yours!

Now, your only task is to start making the recipes that I have shared in this book. No matter where you are in right now, you can enjoy the cuisines from various parts of the world with the help of copycat recipes. Along with the multiple benefits of copycat recipes, you will also be able to customize the dishes according to your choice.

Are you not getting enough time to visit a specialty restaurant? There is nothing to worry about as copycat recipes are here to your rescue. All you need to do now is to pick some new recipes every week and introduce your family to a new cuisine from some corner of the world without even going there in person. The recipes that I have included in this book are specialties of those particular places.

These recipes can serve all your food needs quite well; whether it's your routine meals or a fancy one for a special occasion, you can cook with healthy and organic ingredients to bring good flavors and lots of nutrients to your dinner tables. These are stepping stones for you to master and make these recipes your own by adding your style and twist on these dishes. Enjoy these dishes, and most importantly - have fun!

CPSIA information can be obtained
at www.ICGtesting.com
Printed in the USA
LVHW101234091220
673699LV00010B/131

9 781914 164095